OECD Studies on Water

Implementing Water Economics in the EU Water Framework Directive

OECD
BETTER POLICIES FOR BETTER LIVES

Please cite this publication as:
OECD (2023), *Implementing Water Economics in the EU Water Framework Directive*, OECD Studies on Water, OECD Publishing, Paris, https://doi.org/10.1787/d6abda81-en.

ISBN 978-92-64-69407-1 (print)
ISBN 978-92-64-90922-9 (pdf)
ISBN 978-92-64-41660-4 (HTML)
ISBN 978-92-64-69857-4 (epub)

OECD Studies on Water
ISSN 2224-5073 (print)
ISSN 2224-5081 (online)

Photo credits: Cover © Falling into water droplets By Serg64

Corrigenda to publications may be found on line at: www.oecd.org/about/publishing/corrigenda.htm.

Foreword

A distinctive feature of the European Union's (EU) Water Framework Directive (WFD) is the multiple references to economics. According to the WFD, EU member states are mandated to:

- Recover the financial, environmental and resource costs of using water. These costs include the opportunity cost of using water (which should reflect scarcity), the costs of pollution (in line with the Polluter Pays Principle), and the financial costs of operating infrastructure and services to access water;
- Establish water prices that promote water use efficiency and hence discourage wastage and encourage efficient allocation of water resources;
- Use economic analyses and appropriate data to document costs of measures and investments, their allocation, and the contribution of different water users (households, industry and agriculture) towards cost recovery.

Reference to water economics in the WFD and Flood Directive (FD) resonates with similar references in the OECD Council Recommendation on Water, adopted by OECD member countries in December 2016. It follows that the OECD and the European Commission share a common interest in facilitating the diffusion of water economics and robust practices for cost recovery and diffusion of the Polluter Pays Principle across their constituencies and beyond.

The Fitness Check of the EU's water legislation and the assessment of the second cycle of implementation of river basin management plans and flood risk management plans indicates that there is room for improvements with regard to the integration of water economics into the framework of integrated water management.

The European Commission - DG Environment and the OECD Environment Directorate embarked on a joint project to provide practical guidance to EU members states and support further progress towards robust water economics to inform water resources management. Ultimately, this is expected to facilitate compliance with the WFD and Flood Directives.

Noting that the financing of measures is a major obstacle towards improved implementation, this joint project aimed to: i) assess whether EU member states have set up appropriate mechanisms to recover costs of water management; ii) identify good practices that can inspire further progress in member states; and iii) provide policy and methodological guidance on how to further recover costs of water management. Analyses and policy messages are relevant to a broader audience, with an interest in cost-effective and fair management of water resources.

Acknowledgements

This document reports on a joint project by the European Commission DG Environment and the OECD Environment Directorate. The project included a series of four thematic workshops on various dimensions of the economic pillar of the Water Framework Directive, convened during the first semester of 2022. The Synthesis workshop drew the threads together. Each thematic workshop was informed by a thematic background note; main features of the discussion were captured in discussion highlights. The background notes, the discussion highlights of the four thematic projects are compiled at: https://www.oecd.org/water/dg-env-economics-of-wfd.htm.

The report is an output of the OECD Environment Policy Committee (EPOC) and its Working Party on Working Party on Biodiversity, Water and Ecosystems (WPBWE). The OECD team was coordinated by Xavier Leflaive. Aude Farnault, Marijn Korndewal, Helen Laubenstein, Delia Sanchez Trancon contributed at various stages. Ines Reale provided administrative support. The work was conducted under the overall supervision of Walid Oueslati, Acting Head of the Environment, Transitions and Resilience Division of the OECD's Environment Directorate. The OECD benefitted from active cooperation with and substantial inputs from Acteon, led by Pierre Strosser, with Gloria De Paoli.

The European Commission provided constructive guidance throughout the two-year process. Bettina Doeser is acknowledged for her leadership. Paulus Arnoldus challenged the status quo and helped push the boundaries of economic analyses. He is gratefully acknowledged.

The project and this document were produced with the financial assistance of the European Union. The views expressed herein can in no way be taken to reflect the official opinion of the European Union.

Table of contents

Boxes

Abbreviations and acronyms

CBAs	Cost-Benefits-Analyses
CECs	Contaminants of Emerging Concern
CIS	Common Implementation Strategy
EPR	Extended Producers' Responsibility
FD	Flood Directive
FRMP	Flood Risk Management Plan
JRC	Joint Research Center
LVC	Land-value capture
MCA	Multi-Criteria Analysis
NbS	Nature-Based Solutions
PES	Payment for Ecosystem Services
PPP	Polluter Pays principle
RBMP	River Basin Management Plan
REACH	Registration, Evaluation, Authorisation and Restriction of Chemical
SIPs	Strategic Investment Pathways
TNC	The Nature Conservancy
UWWTD	Urban Wastewater Treatment Directive
WFD	Water Framework Directive
WSS	Water Supply and Sanitation

Executive summary

More than 20 years after its implementation, the European Union (EU) Water Framework Directive (WFD) operates in a new context, mainly characterised by new cost drivers, namely unforeseen increases in the prices of the energy inputs, as well as increasing water scarcity coupled with the increased stringency in regulation stemming from the higher environmental ambitions in the green transition.

The current economic turbulence and acceleration of the green transition exacerbate issues related to the depreciation of existing assets over time, and the capacity to build up a reserve to finance the replacement investments. Energy costs increases can undermine the earning capacity of operators of existing services and thus their capacity to self-finance and attract external private financing for new investments, when the tariff regulation and policies do not allow to pass on these additional operating costs. The same applies for the additional capital costs coming from the investments prompted by the policy ambitions enshrined in the Zero Pollution Action Plan and, more generally, the Green Deal environmental and climate policies.

In such a context, effective implementation of the WFD and the achievement of its ambitions require that due consideration be given to its economic pillar, designed to support a cost-effective implementation for member states and communities. Core features of the economic pillar of the Water Framework Directive include:

Recovery of the financial, as well as the (non-financial) environmental and resource costs of water services. These costs include the opportunity cost of using water (which should reflect scarcity), the costs of pollution and environmental pressures (in line with the Polluter Pays Principle), and the financial costs of operating infrastructure and services to access water;

Water prices that promote water use efficiency and hence discourage wastage and encourage an efficient allocation of water resources;

An adequate contribution of water uses (use sectors) to the recovery of the costs of water services, in the context of growing cost pressures;

Economic analyses and appropriate data to document costs of measures and investments, their allocation, based on the contribution of different water users (households, industry and agriculture) to cost recovery.

The Fitness Check of the EU's water legislation and the assessment of the second cycle of implementation of river basin management plans (RBMPs) and flood risk management plans (FRMPs) indicate that there is considerable room for improvement with regard to the integration of water economics into the framework of integrated water management.

A series of thematic workshops co-convened by the European Commission and the OECD shed some light on some of the challenges EU member states face in relation to the economic pillar of the Water Framework Directive, and options to overcome them. Progress in this direction can accelerate the implementation of the WFD and thus contribute to the achievement of its environmental objectives in a cost-effective and fair manner. It can support better planning and investment decisions, to make the best of available resources and capacities.

The workshops aimed to establish a series of actions that the member states and the European Commission may wish to consider to accelerate the implementation of the WFD, building on a robust economics-based approach.

Cost recovery is a distinctive and foundational feature of the WFD. A high level of (financial) cost recovery reduces the claim on public financial support and promotes access to private finance sources. In addition, pricing can be a signal to incentivise water use efficiency, but with the important qualification that it needs to be embedded in a comprehensive and balanced policy package. The pricing instrument needs to take account of the different levels of price elasticity of water for different uses, which is very low for water use reflecting basic needs. Therefore, pricing instruments need to be accompanied by measures to address affordability. The workshop participants insisted that affordability needs to be thoroughly assessed; and that it is best addressed through targeted social measures than through complex – often regressive – tariff structures.

Polluter Pays principle is at the core of the WFD. Member states face similar challenges with its implementation, in particular as regards the identification of the polluter and its contribution to the pollution into - or the environmental pressure on - the water body in question. These challenges relate to data, methods and scale analysis; they also reflect the difficulties to measure and monetise the benefits of a particular project. These challenges lead to an uneven playing field. Countries would benefit from additional data, guidance and conceptual clarification.

Water scarcity is hardly new in Europe but has recently emerged as a pan-European challenge. This has revived attention to water allocation regimes, which are often inherited from times of plenty and thus in need of reform. Existing guidance on environmental flows needs to be more thoroughly implemented; clear definitions and stringent enforcement can help. Water allocation regimes are expected to deliver better results in combination with water scarcity pricing and the spare capacity from alternative sources to be used during peak scarcity. The workshops highlighted the complex dynamics of water use efficiency: when rebound effects are not factored in and specified in water allocation regimes, measures to enhance water use efficiency may not lead to water savings and hence not benefit water resources and the communities downstream.

In a context characterised by mounting uncertainties about water availability and use as well as the exposure and vulnerability to water risks, investment decisions would benefit from better **planning**. In particular, member states would benefit from more guidance on scenario analyses, in particular in relation to climate change and associated crises. Planning could also be improved by supplementing project level analysis with those at the level of strategic investment pathways.

When it comes to **finance** for measures and water-related investment, new sources of finance could be attracted through fair risk-sharing arrangements. Workshop participants agreed they could revive past discussions on a series of measures that can harness new sources of finance. They mentioned:

Depreciation methods that can be designed to serve policy objectives while adequately contributing to the desired rate of cost recovery for water services (with more or less stringent pressure on capacities to generate cashflows). The issue has become even more relevant in the context marked by high inflation rates;

Land-value capture, as a financing instrument that can translate some of the value added by achieving good water status into a revenue stream, thereby triggering the possibility to finance programmes of measures or water-related investment;

Extended producer's responsibility, as a new frontier of making polluters pay and stimulating green innovation, for instance in relation to contaminants of emerging concern.

Most of the actions suggested for discussion have a strong cross-sectoral dimension, reflecting the message that further implementation of the WFD – including its economic pillar - requires collaboration across sectors, specifically those that affect water availability and demand as well as exposure and vulnerability to water risks (sanitation, agriculture, land use and urban development, fluvial transportation, energy generation have been discussed during the thematic workshops).

The pervasive under-valuation of the resource and benefits associated with investment in water by both public and private actors constrains financing opportunities. One pending issue relates to the assumption of its unlimited supply by many economic sectors. The proper valuation of water is a precondition for the planning of measures and investments and their prioritisation, as well as monetisation as a basis for designing pricing instruments and adequate contributions from water user groups. The latter is also a requirement for developing much needed innovative financing instruments.

Another pending issue is the appropriate geographical scale to design and implement programmes of measures. The WFD takes the river basin district as the geographical basis for the programming. However, it appears that measures, which are beneficial at a particular scale, may not be optimal at another scale. Moreover, the outcome of cost-benefit analysis of a measure may vary according to the geographical scale of the analysis. It is not clear how to reconcile actions across geographical scales: mainstream tools for economic analysis, such as cost-benefit analysis, are not adequate to address this issue.

The new context outlined above calls for a reconsideration of price, investment and depreciation arrangements. It may also involve defining a different level of the recovery of the costs of water services (as allowed by article 9(1)). In addition, workshop participants made pertinent observations that the application of the Polluter Pays Principle in the cost recovery efforts seems in practice geared towards compensation for incurred pollution costs, rather than the avoidance of polluting activities.

In the new context, the need for increasingly stringent – and potentially costly – environmental policies (such as the WFD) shows the importance of cost-recovery arrangements while posing pertinent questions on the current cost-recovery arrangements, namely to a large extent relying on recuperating costs through – limited – water bills and charges. Preliminary discussions on land-value capture and extended producer responsibility indicate a promising potential to widen the basis of cost recovery that also provide adequate incentives and deliver a more just and equitable distribution of the costs.

Background and rationale

A distinctive feature of the Water Framework Directive (WFD) is the multiple references to economic aspects. According to the WFD, members of the European Union (EU) are mandated to:

Recover the financial, environmental and resource costs of using water. These costs include the financial costs of operating infrastructure and services to access water the (non-financial) costs of pollution, in the prevailing interpretation comprising all environmental pressures (in line with the Polluter Pays Principle), and the opportunity cost of using water (which should reflect scarcity);

Establish water prices that promote water use efficiency and hence discourage wastage and encourage efficient allocation of water resources;

Define the size of the adequate contributions to the costs of water services that the various water user sectors need to incur;

Use economic analysis on a robust base of appropriate data to document costs of measures and investments, their allocation;

Identify the cost-effective combination of measures that can achieve good status.

The Fitness Check of the EU's water legislation and the assessment of the second cycle of implementation of river basin management plans (RBMPs) and flood risk management plans (FRMPs) indicates that there is room for improvement with regard to the integration of water economics into the frame of integrated water management:

Financing is a major obstacle towards improved implementation. For the WFD, the objectives of the Programmes of Measures are mostly determined by what can be delivered with the pre-set available budgets informed by the policies that are already in place. For the FD, the financing of measures is not specified in the Flood Risk Management Plans;

Much of the potential of cost recovery is left untapped. One third of the countries only apply cost recovery to water supply and sanitation services. Several countries are progressively applying cost recovery to a wider range of water uses, including hydropower generation, navigation, flood protection, or self-abstraction for agriculture and industry. In addition, "the adequate contribution" of certain water uses to the recovery of water services' costs remains low to non-existent;

The estimation of actual and future investment needs does not always deliver reliable figures for a robust investment planning. The methodologies and scope differ and often lack transparency. Financial costs are the focus of the cost recovery efforts, even though the methods used may not fully account for costs (in particular as regards capital and depreciation costs). Less attention is devoted to wider economic costs. Only half of EU member countries document the opportunity / scarcity costs of using water and the (non-financial) pollution costs;

The estimation of costs and benefits is insufficiently documented, and exemptions based on "disproportionate costs" are not always properly justified;

The use of cost-effectiveness analysis could further be improved in order to increase the efficiency the implementation of the necessary measures.

Further progress towards a more robust water economics approach to support water resource management is needed to facilitate compliance with the WFD and FD objectives. While finance is often referred to by countries as a constraint in the implementation efforts, a better use of insights from water economics can ensure that available financial resources are used effectively (i.e. allocated to measures that contribute tangible benefits on the ground in terms of good ecological status) and that potential sources of revenues are mobilised.

With this in mind, the European Commission – DG Environment and the OECD Environment Directorate endeavoured to:

Explore what could be appropriate mechanisms, including those hitherto rather underused, to recover costs of water management;

identify good practices that can inspire further progress in member states; and

provide policy and methodological guidance as to how to further recover costs of water management.

This effort took the form of a series of 4 thematic workshops, organised by the OECD and hosted by the European Commission. The 4 thematic workshops focused respectively on the implementation of the Polluter Pays principle; cost recovery; water scarcity, and the water-related investment planning and financing. A concluding, fifth workshop focused on cross-cutting issues.

Discussions at each workshop were supported by a background note from the OECD on the policy issues, available information, and selected good practices in Europe, OECD countries or beyond. Each workshop was organised to facilitate the exchange of experience and to overcome some of the bottlenecks to further documenting costs, supporting cost recovery and allocating efforts across water users. Invitations were sent to the appropriate members of the Common Implementation Strategy plus other relevant experts, as well as the members of the OECD Working Party on Biodiversity Water and Ecosystems. Discussions highlights are appended to this report and have informed the executive summary.

The next section reports on some of the cross-cutting messages that emerged from the series of thematic and concluding workshops.

Cross-cutting issues

Lack of or patchy data, discomfort with methodologies have been recurrently mentioned as obstacles to robust decision-making. While some participants questioned the extent to which actual decisions are informed by the (mandatory) economic analysis and data, there was an agreement that the implementation of the WFD would benefit from improvements in these domains. Of note: participants deliberately stayed away from issues with definitions, are these are best addressed in other fora.

Methods and tools for economic assessment and investment planning

Economic assessments are required to support robust and effective investment planning. Participants note that a lot of money is going into the water sector, but it is not always sure whether it is best used to the benefit of the water uses and, more generally, communities.

Typically, investment planning still builds on previous experience and years, a backward-looking approach increasingly at odds with the imminent challenges to and policy demands on the water sector. This is unlikely to lead to robust decisions as i) we do not know whether past investment levels and strategies were appropriate and up to the already fully defined challenges; and ii) a new context has emerged: it is characterised by more uncertainties about water availability and demand, increased water-related risks, increased costs triggered by more stringent environmental policies, the need to adapt to climate change, and most recently a more challenging economic context. It follows that relying on past experience is unlikely to inform robust investment decisions. The workshop revealed a great interest in a better use of scenario-analysis to take account of the prevalent uncertainties, namely multiple scenarios.

Valuable economic assessments would benefit from methods and tools to characterise good adaptation to climate change and resilient policies and infrastructures. A first step is to develop robust water balances in order to understand how much water is available and can be allocated to competing uses (including the environment). The WFD (Annex III) requires a long-term projection of both water supply and demand as the basis of the economic analysis. Consequently, some guidance on water allocation regimes and e-flows has been developed under the Common Implementation Strategy (CIS), but more work is required to overcome ambiguities and support implementation. Future work under the Working Group on Water Scarcity and Droughts is topical and timely.

Moreover, a challenge is to combine more robust scenarios about climate change and its impacts on water availability and use, with the appropriate level of disaggregation of data to support action. On-going and future work of DG CLIMA is topical here. Risks of maladaptation are significant and can derive from poorly designed CBAs and high discount rates.

Planning and investment are also hampered by the transboundary nature of quite a few water bodies and the need to coordinate action across administrative borders. The workshops have touched on the issue occasionally, and it needs to be more systematically factored in. The transboundary nature of water flows affects the capacity to derive robust economic analyses: the costs and benefits of a programme of measures often do not stop at administrative boundaries and should be assessed at basin or aquifer level.

It follows that CBAs (Cost-Benefits-Analyses) usually fail to satisfactorily account for physical and ecosystem reality. Moreover, different countries value water differently; and use different economic policy instruments for water management and related issues.

Different EU member states have different experience with a variety of policy instruments. As regards economic policy instruments, for instance, experience varies in relation to access and use of EU Funding instruments; the number, level and structure of charges collected by water agencies; how water, soil and biodiversity are connected in institutions and policies. A lot could be gained by more systematically sharing about the multiple instruments, the details of fees and taxes, methods and ways in which economic assessments are developed[1].

The ambivalence of prevalent economic assumptions – the case of water-use efficiency and increasing block tariffs

The case of water use efficiency illustrates some of the limitations of prevalent economic analyses when applied to water. Another illustration derives from the analyses of tariff structures for water supply and sanitation services.

Issues with water use efficiency as a response to water scarcity

Water use efficiency seems to be an obvious response to water scarcity and contribution to good status of water bodies (both surface and groundwater). In Europe, policy efforts seem to bear fruit as the overall water use efficiency is increasing: for instance, total water abstraction for agriculture is going down and water use per hectare has decreased from 557mm to 382mm, driven by precision irrigation, higher costs of using water, water quotas and other measures.

In practice, the situation is more complex. First, experience shows that, if not properly captured in water allocation regimes, water saved through efficiency measures rarely benefit the environment and communities downstream. Quite on the contrary, efficiency measures can lead to an extension of irrigated area and / or a shift towards more water-intensive uses (including more thirsty crops). Such rebound effects can enhance the dependence on stable water flows and reduce / weaken the resilience of water systems to climate risks. It needs to be controlled, through the definition of return flows, curtailing water rights (to reflect efficiency gains), or limits to the surface of land that can be irrigated. In addition, the use of pricing and alternative sources of supply in times of scarcity contribute to stabilising the water demand over time in an efficient manner.

In Europe, while water abstraction for agriculture is going down, overall water consumption remains stable. And energy use increases. This aggregate vision masks huge discrepancies at across countries.

Limitations of increasing block tariffs

During the workshops, several countries have shared their experience with increasing block tariffs to manage demand for water and to generate revenues to cover the costs of service provision. Increasing-block tariffs provide water for basic needs at a lower price. They can be progressive when they meet two conditions:

- highest tariff blocks are set well above the average cost of service provision and income generated serves to cover the costs of the subsidised lower block; and
- they take into consideration that poor households can actually consume more water than wealthy ones (because they have larger families, or less water-efficient networks or appliances).

In practice, well-targeted tariff structures are complicated and may be perceived as opaque. They require information on water use and household features (for instance on the size of households, age and physical conditions of individuals) that are usually not accessible to service providers. This explains why sophisticated tariff structures can fail to target the households most in need: while authorities and service providers allocate considerable amounts of time and efforts to designing and adjusting tariff structures to accommodate multiple policy objectives, they usually fail to combine efficiency and equity objectives.

Moreover, the efficiency of tariffs as instruments to manage domestic water demand depends on households' response to price signals. The literature suggests that this response is usually limited, in particular in the short term. Accompanying measures, such as transparent water bills and nudging, can enhance the elasticity of domestic water demand to price.

Equity and Environmental justice in the context of the WFD

Environmental justice and equity emerged several times in the course of the workshops. As the point above suggests, poorly designed tariffs for water services – most frequently in the case of sophisticated tariff structures – may trigger equity issues when poor households still face affordability issues for what constitutes an essential service. This problem may exacerbate with increasing water stress and resulting higher water tariffs. Persistent large gaps in the price of water services across the broad water user sectors (households, industry, agriculture), even when allowed by policy-makers for a long time, may at some point trigger equity questions in the political domain. Similarly, policymakers may also be increasingly confronted with equity arguments as regards the divergence in water price across regions, that follows from persistent differences in water availability. Finally, any investment backlog or failure to properly operate and maintain existing assets transfers risks and financial burden to the next generation(s), raising intergenerational equity issues.

It follows that decisions on the level and structure of tariffs for water services should reflect thorough analyses of distributional issues and also consider the use of flanking policy instruments outside of the water policy domain. For instance, rather than moving to more uniform water prices over regions differing in the degree of water scarcity, policy makers could consider countervailing financial transfers in the form of investments in water efficiency.

Discussions at the workshops also reported situations where financing stringent environmental policies through water bills can disproportionately affect small communities, who contribute relatively modestly to overall water pollution. One option to address this issue, is to consider financing arrangements that provide targeted support to small communities' investments in abatement and prevention, in particular in view of the usually relatively difficult access and expertise of private finance. Aggregating water services at a larger geographical scale or affecting fiscal revenues to wastewater collection and treatment can be parts of the solution.

More generally, it is not clear how the WFD and its core principles take into account unequal exposure and vulnerability to risks of poor status of water bodies. Urban and rural communities, upstream and downstream areas will be affected in different ways. In the new context sketched above, a thorough assessment of how these discrepancies are factored in the WFD would seem relevant.

Potential next steps

Based on the discussions with member states and stakeholders, the following initiatives could be explored to support member states' efforts to comply with the ambition of the WFD, by 2027 and beyond.

1. Launch a dedicated call under Joint Programming Initiative on "Water challenges for a changing world" to research on methodologies and methods for planning river basin measures under uncertainty, in particular factoring in climate change. The call would cover the use of disaggregated climate data, alternative economic methods to support decision making under uncertainty (such as cost-benefit analysis, production function, behavioural economics, the modelling of the water economy combining the pricing and investment instruments), guidance for scenario analyses, and tools and metrics to combine or sequence measures in consistent and cost-effective programmes;
2. Make an inventory of economic policy instruments used by member states to fund water activities, or aimed to signal the opportunity cost of using water and make water pollution and other negative externalities costly. This project could build on the work published by the European Commission "Economic data related to the implementation of the WFD and the FD and the financing of measures" by looking at the destination of the collected revenues and the potential of new instruments, such as eco-schemes, land-value capture or taxes on impervious surfaces. This work could be expanded and completed by collecting data directly from member states instead of relying on publicly available data. The OECD database on Policy Instruments for the Environment (PINE) could be used as a platform, possibly supplementing data from non-European OECD countries;
3. Explore the opportunities for - and potential modalities of - innovative financing mechanisms for measures in line with the environmental objectives of the WFD. Two instruments stand out, based on discussions at the thematic workshops:
    a. Extended producers' responsibility (EPR). The instrument could be designed and pilot-tested for one set of issues affecting water quality in one country or river basin, for a particular industry[2]. Based on discussions at the workshops, potential countries could be France, Germany, or the Netherlands, where the water sector has built relationships with other sectors such as chemical industry including pharmaceuticals, or agriculture. Work on a transboundary basin would be challenging but most relevant;
    b. Land-value capture (LVC), as a fiscal instrument that can discourage activities that increase exposure and vulnerability to water risks, and potentially finance measures that contribute to good status of a water body. While experience abounds with LVC to finance transport infrastructures, track record for water-related assets is limited. The work could take stock of recent experience in Europe and globally, assess bottlenecks for further deployment of LVC as a financing instrument for investments in line with the WFD ambition across EU member states, and explore options to address these bottlenecks. Issues related to valuing water and the multiple benefits of water security would play a prominent role;
4. Develop a series of workshops on water scarcity and climate change, to explore measures that can help mitigate scarcity risks without detrimental effects on the good status of water bodies. Such measures would include:

- scarcity pricing;
- robust water allocation regimes, which factor in "non-traditional users" (e.g., energy generation, navigation), e-flows and return flows;
- better use of forecasting and modelling capacities for decision making;
- stimulating demand for reclaimed water (through a combination of water quality standards, water entitlements and pricing measures) as well as determining its efficient place in the "water supply mix"; and
- appropriate and adequate policy instruments for an efficient use of storage: the planning of its capacity (in context of the whole range of water supply options); its allocation over users and over time in combination with costing and pricing measures; and distinctive challenges when storage also serves as reservoir for hydropower generation.

The series of workshops would build on the experience of member states (most specifically from the Mediterranean region) and from non-European OECD members such as Australia, Chile, or Israel, with long experience with water scarcity. The workshops would be informed by thematic background notes. They would supplement the work undertaken with the CIS WG Economics and ATG on water scarcity and drought; they can involve cooperation with DG CLIMA, DG AGRI and JRC.

1. Develop a series of workshops on the climate impacts on soil, as a common threat for agriculture, water resources management and nature protection and restoration. These workshops could identify common threats, explore solutions and potential trade-offs across the three policy areas (climate, agriculture and water). This workshop could build on - and support - the new EU context (CAP 2023-2027, Nature Restoration Law, Green Deal and Nature Based Solutions);
2. Prospective work on the concept and definition of "good status", taking account of climate change and emerging trends in water use and pressures on water bodies. The WFD was designed almost 25 years ago. Since then, new knowledge on climate change, contaminants of emerging concern and other issues have arisen. While the Fitness Check confirmed that the WFD is both sufficiently prescriptive and flexible enough, foresight could revisit some of the core pillars of the economics of the WFD and associated guidance, and discuss how relevant they might be beyond 2027 (and towards 2050). Joint work between the OECD and the European Commission would be most timely, valuable, inspirational, and impactful, in Europe and globally. It could build on Joint Research Centre's modelling capacities, on-going OECD work on losses and damages from climate change (and uncertainties in climate modelling) and the experience of EU and OECD member states.

Notes

[1] France has developed a methodology for the economic analysis of disproportionate cost, based on a tool that facilitates the use of economic analysis at sub-sovereign level. Water agencies use it when preparing the Programme of Measures. The tool is being updated for the fourth River Basin Management Plans by a group of practitioners and environmental economists. The main goals are to update values for existing benefits and new monetised benefits, make the assessment more robust, and make the tool more user friendly (see the highlight of the workshop on the Polluter Pays principle for more information).

[2] Note that this echoes with a European Commission's proposal, in the context of the revision of the Urban Waste Water Treatment Directive.

1 Cost Recovery

Cost recovery is a foundational feature of the WFD. It relates to issues of fairness, the effectiveness of public expenditures and the creditworthiness of water service providers. Pricing and measures to address affordability concerns are covered in the chapter. An emerging question is whether cost recovery remains a viable option in the future.

The thematic workshop is part of a series aimed to facilitate the implementation of the economics of the WFD in European Member States. It gathered around 70 participants, including government representatives, water utilities, associations of water utilities and regulators, research institutions, NGOs and Directorate Generals (European Commission).

The workshop, co-convened by the OECD and the European Commission - DG ENV, focused on cost recovery. It aimed at:

- Exchanging experience and knowledge on water-pricing mechanisms designed to trigger efficient water uses and recover costs;
- Raising awareness of affordability issues related to cost recovery, and ways to address them;
- Identifying and disseminating good practices and emerging approaches related to efficient and innovative cost recovery mechanisms, to unlock untapped sources of revenues;
- Reflecting on cost recovery mechanisms for water management in the context of increasingly stringent environmental policies.

Speakers with diverse backgrounds shared their experiences related to cost recovery and the WFD goals. Highlights of the discussions are provided below. The agenda, a background note and speakers' slides are available on the meeting webpage.

Key messages

Session 1: Water-pricing mechanisms

Adequate incentive pricing

- Ideally, water should pay for water and water charges or tariffs for water services should reflect all costs incurred in a single bill (price signal). In reality, tariffs do not reflect all costs (due to initial subsidies, low maintenance, opportunity cost difficult to recover, among others) and tariffs seek to achieve many and sometimes conflicting objectives (cost recovery, inclusive access, water savings...).
- Price elasticity of water uses depends on many factors (including the tariff structure, the initial price level, the time frame, the magnitude of change, the type of water use...). Water pricing should be embedded in a set of measures to achieve all its objectives, particularly water savings. Thus, water pricing is a complex tool to use as an incentive for saving water.
- While pricing can sometimes be an effective incentive to save water, reducing consumption can cause significant problems for operators. Thus, water utilities have no incentive to encourage water saving.

Addressing affordability

- Affordability problems are better addressed through targeted social measures, rather than social tariffs. First, affordability is not merely a water issue: it is essentially a poverty issue and needs to be addressed as such. Second, low tariffs usually benefit the well-off and not the poorest. Moreover, designing effective social tariffs can be complicated; it may miss the target, especially in the absence of accurate data on household composition and revenues.
- Nonetheless, social measures are not always efficient and sometimes difficult to implement (difficulties to target and reach people, administrative costs of data access, difficult negotiations with social actors...). Furthermore, targeted social measures only apply if a robust social system is in place.

- If there is a consensus that targeted social measures are more appropriate than social tariffs, what prevents countries from recovering costs through water bills? Participants mentioned the lack of willingness to pay (which can be addressed thanks to accompanying measures, among others) and political considerations related to tariff setting (underlying the benefit of an independent economic regulator for water supply and sanitation - WSS).

Depreciation methods

- Financial depreciation of existing assets is complex and methods vary across jurisdictions. The way depreciation is calculated affects tariffs and cost recovery rates. The issue is particularly topical for assets funded by EU grants.
- Each depreciation method has potential advantages and disadvantages, considering the financeability of required capital maintenance, incentives for efficient investment and allowing for affordable and equitable bills. It raises key question of how disadvantages can be lessened, with potential for consideration of hybrid options. Intergenerational equity matters.

Session 2: Efficient (innovative) cost-recovery mechanisms

- Apart from abstraction and pollution, charges on other pressures represent a very small percentage of the total funding for water management in the EU. These instruments have an untapped potential for raising additional funds for water management. A large variety of charges are implemented by countries, which would require efforts of harmonisation.
- Land value capture (LVC) is a policy approach that enables communities to recover and reinvest land value increases that result from public investment and government actions. LVC is attractive from a public finance point of view (from an efficiency and an equity perspective), but under-used in the water sector, with too little peer-learning across countries. LVC has a lot of potential for climate action, and could be applied in the water sector as water infrastructures can have a positive impact on land value. Participants mentioned examples of applications in Australia, South Korea and Morocco.

Session 3: How fit is cost recovery for the future?

- With the Zero Pollution Action Plan, the course of direction is clearly towards more stringency, driven by several environmental Directives. While it intends to minimise damage, increasing the level of stringency of environmental policy will increase costs of meeting environmental requirements for society. The magnitude of the additional cost will reflect efficiency of policy responses.
- The implications for customers of funding environmental improvements through water charges can differ significantly depending on industry structure. The costs per customer served of meeting environmental improvements can vary significantly depending on the supply circumstances. This is perhaps most obvious when the provision of services to sparsely populated areas is considered (e.g. Estonia and Lithuania), as there is a steep cost-curve associated with low-scale.
- More stringent environmental requirements may deliver benefits to a population that is much wider than that of the plant they may be applied to. Where regional averaging is applied, the distribution of costs (through charges) may align with the distribution of benefits. This is less so when the WSS industry is fragmented and compliance costs are borne by small communities. Consolidation (at least of payments for environmental improvements) may be important to allow for a better alignment between the costs and benefits of meeting requirements.

Next steps

Participants indicated the following next steps as priority:

- Facilitating peer learning between Member states and information sharing (through dedicated workshops, platforms, publications...) on water saving incentive mechanisms and depreciation methods in relation to cost recovery, affordability and intergenerational equity;
- Sharing more information on the list of uses / pressures that could be targeted by charges on other pressures, the scope of such instruments, good practices and implementation guidance;
- Promoting peer learning between countries on LVC and its potential benefits in the water sector;
- Furthering the discussion on appropriate scales and levels of consolidation of WSS services with regards to cost recovery and the financing of increasingly stringent environmental policies.

Session 1: Water-pricing mechanisms

The approach to water-pricing should consider multiple roles/objectives:

1. Consistency with the recovery of efficiently incurred costs, including capital expenditure (CAPEX), to the extent that it remains to be recovered from customers;
1. The financeability of future investment requirements: providing a robust basis upon which utilities can fund investments viewed as appropriate and desirable;
2. Efficiency incentives: providing incentives to deliver appropriate performance levels, cost efficiently over time;
3. Allowing for affordable, acceptable and equitable bills: while this can clearly raise broader social and political considerations, it is important to recognise the various implications that different tariffs setting approaches have in relation to these matters.

These objectives are not always compatible with one another, making the choice and implementation of 'appropriate' water-pricing mechanisms challenging.

Adequate incentive pricing: what is an 'efficient' water-pricing mechanism (triggering efficient water uses)?

Price elasticity of water uses depends on many factors, including the tariff structure, the initial price level, the time frame, the magnitude of change, the type of water use, the presence of alternative resources, and users' income, among others. Therefore, for water charges or tariffs to drive demand, they should be embedded in a set of measures.

In France, water agencies collect a tax to preserve water resources, but it is too low to encourage water-saving behaviour. In the French collective irrigation systems, there is a very large diversity of tariffs, but three of them represent 2/3 of the tariffs: flat rate (26% of the cases, mainly for gravity irrigation systems), two-parts tariffs (35% of the cases, with a fixed part based on the irrigation surface and the rest based on the outflow or volume consumed), and (purely) proportional tariffs (5%, small structures). Two-part tariffs and proportional tariffs theoretically provide incentives for water savings as there is a relationship between the payment and the amount of water used. On the contrary, most of the new collective irrigation systems in France use flat rates and therefore do not have incentive water pricing (they generally invest in water metering only after 15 to 20 years of operation, after reimbursing their initial investment) [1].

Participants shared the view that, while pricing can sometimes be effective to incentivise water savings, reducing consumption can lead to significant (financial) issues for operators. For instance, in Romania, prices increased for WSS in the early 2000s and in parallel consumption decreased significantly, which triggered significant issues for water utilities. Furthermore, participants pointed out that prices generally increase when consumers decrease their consumptions (due to high fixed costs). Thus, reducing consumption would not be in the interest of the operator and the consumer (because of rising costs). Participants also drew a parallel with energy utilities, which have incentives to promote energy savings. This difference could be explained by the fact that the price elasticity could be higher for the energy sector, because energy represents a larger share of the household budget.

Addressing affordability: what are the pros and cons of social measures vis-à-vis social tariffs?

Financial sustainability, environmental sustainability and affordability are three different imperatives that are difficult to reconcile only through water tariffs. Addressing affordability just through the 'expenditure / income ratio' can be problematic. It can raise questions of affordability thresholds, notably in relation to other basic goods (affordability is not just a water issue). Thus, affordability problems are better addressed through targeted social measures, rather than social tariffs. Moreover, designing effective social tariffs can be complicated. Social tariffs may miss the target, especially without precise data on revenues of households. Nonetheless, when social measures are lacking, different approaches are possible: tariff design (social tariffs, increasing block tariffs – being phased out because missing the target, free block of water), payment support (Water Solidarity Funds, facilitated payments), and addressing consumption (awareness-raising).

Participants generally agreed that affordability issues should be addressed through social measures rather than social tariffs, otherwise it could jeopardize the sustainability of water utilities, but raised the point that social measures are not always efficient and sometimes difficult to implement. For instance, some cities in France have faced difficulties to support low-income groups with social measures (difficult to target and reach people, administrative costs of data access, difficult negotiations with social actors to access data...). To address them, the French authorities have issued a toolkit for water social policies compiling guidelines and best practices (available at https://www.ecologie.gouv.fr/favoriser-lacces-leau-tous-politique-sociale-leau). Furthermore, targeted social measures only apply if a robust social system is in place, which is most often the case in Europe.

Depreciation methods: How depreciation might be 'flexed' to assist with financeability / cost recovery concerns?

The financial treatment of depreciation of existing assets is a complex issue that varies among water utilities within and between Member States. The way depreciation is calculated affects differently the tariffs and cost recovery rates, and can have particularly significant implications for assets funded by EU grants. Depreciation methods can be calculated from the perspective of spreading the payment of incurred costs (linear depreciation) or financing capital maintenance and renewal (with two main approaches: current cost depreciation and 'pay as you go').

In essence, different methods either reflect the costs incurred to build the assets (in the case of granted assets, that cost is null); or reflect the projected costs to renew existing assets (independently from the actual cost of building existing assets). The former put more pressure on regulated service providers for cost-efficiency, but may trigger a financing gap in the future. The latter generate more revenues for future investment, but relax pressure on operational efficiency and increase water bills, potentially exacerbating affordability issues. Hybrid methods would allow accelerated depreciation under certain conditions that reflect policy priorities.

In the case of Romania, water infrastructure was built mainly with the support of the EU. Royalties of regional operators should ideally reflect the value of the depreciation of public fixed assets, but this is actually the case for only 7 or 8 regional operators out of 44, due to invocation of affordability issues.

Ensuring the sustainability of this infrastructure, and meeting the new EU standards, will require additional financial resources in the medium and long term. The idea is to better reflect depreciation in the water tariffs by widening the implementation and increasing royalties gradually. Affordability issues are to be addressed through different means: regionalization of the water services, cross-subsidies between large and small agglomerations, cost optimization, reduction of leakages, support for vulnerable persons, etc.

In Ireland, the water economic regulator sets the "allowed revenue" for Irish Water (the national public utility) for each revenue control period (around 5 years). This allowed revenue includes a component for operational expenditure, depreciation and for a return on capital (rate of return/return on assets). The depreciation approach is based on a straight line method founded on the expected economic life of the assets. This is allocated to domestic customers (77%) and to non-domestic (23%). Central Government covers a generous allowance for domestic customers from general taxation and only excess uses are charged.

In Lithuania, EU granted assets are not taken into consideration in calculating depreciation and tariffs, which amounts to giving a preference to current rather than future customers. Without taking EU grant into consideration, the cost recovery rate is 100%.

The following next steps were identified during the workshop:

- Facilitating peer learning between Member states and information sharing (through dedicated workshops, platforms, publications…) on water saving incentive mechanisms;
- Share experience with depreciation methods in relation to cost recovery, affordability and intergenerational equity, in a range of policy contexts.

Resources shared by participants

- Aqua Publica Europea (2016), Water Affordability Public Operators' views and approaches on tackling water poverty, https://www.aquapublica.eu/sites/default/files/document/file/ape_water_affordability_final_0.pdf
- EurEau (2017), The Economic Challenge of Reduced Water Consumption https://www.eureau.org/documents/economics-and-legal-affairs/position-papers-2/138-consumption-reduction-january2017/file
- EurEau (2016), Making the human right to water and sanitation a reality in Europe - The role of affordability mechanisms, https://www.eureau.org/documents/drinking-water/position-papers/99-making-the-right-to-water-and-sanitation-reality-europe-september2016/file
- Hoque, S. and R. Hope (2019), Examining the Economics of Affordability Through Water Diaries in Coastal Bangladesh, https://doi.org/10.1142/S2382624X19500115

Session 2: Efficient (innovative) cost-recovery mechanisms

Widening the implementation of water charges and unlocking untapped (private) sources of finance through innovating funding arrangements (including Payments for Ecosystem Services, Extended Producer Responsibility, or fiscal policies based on the Beneficiary Pays principle, such as land value capture mechanisms) can improve cost recovery for water services.

Charges on other pressures on water (beyond abstraction and pollution): should they be further exploited and how?

Charges on other significant pressures on water, beyond abstraction and pollution, mainly target hydromorphological pressures, including inland waterway transport, sediment extraction and obstacles in river bodies. Hydromorphological pressures are the main reasons for failing to reach good status for water bodies. Yet, charges on other pressures represent a very small percentage of the total funding for water management in the EU. They include a large diversity of instruments: water metering fee (Malta, Austria), flow continuity disruption (Bulgaria, France), alluvial sediment extraction (Portugal, Slovenia, Sweden), storm damage tax (Denmark), hydropower production (France, Spain, Slovakia, Slovenia), water restitution fee (France, Italia), contribution to mountain communities, fee for the management of protected areas (Italia), navigation, hydraulic fee, flood protection tax (France), water system management (Netherlands), heart recovery, aquaculture, fishing in commercial ponds, operation of ports, operation of bathing areas (Slovenia). Slovenia is the country targeting the most significant water uses, with a variety of charges in place. Such instruments have an untapped potential for raising additional funds for water management.

Participants discussed the reasons why charges on other pressures were not more widely used, with potential explanations related to transaction costs and difficulty to monitor and implement them. Participants also underlined the ambiguity of the definitions of water users, uses, services and beneficiaries, under the WFD, with a broad scope of possible interpretations. This ambiguity can reflect lack of political agreement but also the actual difficulties in implementing and defining concepts. Participants finally questioned the relevance of earmarking in this context, emphasizing that it can have benefits but also potentially affect the efficiency of public expenditures.

How to unlock untapped sources of revenues to achieve cost recovery? Focus on Land value capture

Land value capture (LVC) is a policy approach that enables communities to recover and reinvest land value increases that result from public investment and government actions. The beneficiaries of public investments that valorise their land or property should return part of their benefit to the public. LVC is an instrument attractive from a public finance point of view, as it is potentially efficient and equitable. It is however under-used to finance water, with too little peer-learning across countries.

Five main LVC instruments can be distinguished: infrastructure levy, developers obligation, charges for development rights, land adjustments and strategic land management. Some instruments are used more than others, with variation among regions of the world (e.g. infrastructure levy less used in low-income countries). The implementation of LVC is challenging, politically and administratively, with obstacles such as resistance from property owners, lack of administrative capacity, low quality of cadastre or land registry, inadequate legal framework or charges too high for owners / developers. On the contrary, there are enabling factors for LVC, including alignment to economic development and planning, political support, enabling framework (law, policy), technical capacity, and institutional mechanisms. LVC has a lot of potential for climate action, and could be applied in the water sector as water infrastructures can have a positive impact on land value. Participants mentioned examples of applications in Australia, South Korea and Morocco.

Participants indicated as priority the following next steps:

- Exploring challenges and opportunities for a wider implementation of charges on other pressures, beyond abstraction and pollution;
- Exploring opportunities and challenges of implementing LVC in the water sector. Promoting peer learning between countries on LVC and its potential for water finance.

Resources shared by participants

- Shampanier, K., N. Mazar and D. Ariely (2007), Zero as a Special Price: The True Value of Free Products, Marketing Science, https://people.duke.edu/~dandan/webfiles/PapersPI/Zero%20as%20a%20Special%20Price.pdf

Session 3: How fit is cost recovery for the future?

Which implications of the zero pollution strategy on cost recovery for water management? Can (or should) increasingly stringent environmental policies be financed through water bills or water-related charges?

While Member States keep struggling to recover some of the costs of their programme of measures, it is clear that costs are likely to increase in the future, driven by the need to address the increasing investment backlog and such drivers as the need to adapt to a changing climate and more stringent environmental and health regulations supported by social expectations. It is not clear how these constraints can be reconciled in practice. What is the appropriate level of stringency for environmental policies? How much can water policy instruments support future costs? The point is not to question cost recovery as such, but to explore whether it remains practical in the emerging context in Europe.

Recovering the costs of programmes of measures through water bills or water-specific economic policy instruments could be questioned in terms of equity. Equity issues may have been masked when past investments benefitted from transfers from the international community. They may emerge more explicitly as communities face the burden of renewing granted assets or funding more stringent environmental and health policies in the future. This may tilt the discussion towards political and practical limits of raising tariffs (or water-related charges) and considering more substantial financial contributions from communities who generated the issues to be addressed through programmes of measures.

In Spain, subsidies for water management are justified for several reasons: fostering cross-subsidies across users and territories, compensating small and medium communities for the high costs related to the absence of economies of scale and encouraging / rewarding environmental benefits (similarly to Payments for Ecosystem services) which go above meeting legal environmental obligations.

With the Zero Pollution Action Plan, the level of environmental ambition at the EU level will increase. Indeed, the course of direction is clearly towards more stringency, driven by several directives including the Urban Waste Water Treatment Directive (UWWTD), the Drinking Water Directive, the Bathing Water Directive and Environmental Quality Standards. This new ambition is pushing towards a wider implementation of the Polluter-Pays Principle. Increasing the level of stringency of environmental policy will increase costs of meeting environmental requirements for society, but it will also avoid larger damage to society. Indeed, the objective of the Zero Pollution Action Plan is ultimately to reduce costs for society. Furthermore, as the efficiency of provision of WSS should have increased over time, the unit cost may have decreased. Thus, the cost of reaching environmental requirements should not increase that much.

The implications for customers of funding environmental improvements through water charges can differ significantly depending on WSS industry structure. The costs per customer can vary significantly depending on circumstances. This is perhaps most obvious in the case of provision of services to sparsely populated areas (e.g. Estonia and Lithuania)

More stringent environmental requirements may deliver benefits to a population that is much wider than water users (those who pay water bills). Where regional averaging is applied, the distribution of costs (through charges) may align closely with the distribution of benefits. This is less the case when the WSS industry is fragmented and smaller groups of users have to pay bills for broader policies on water quality. Under more fragmented structures, applying an approach that appears cost-reflective may result in customers of some companies facing a disproportionately high cost/benefit ratio. Industry and charging structures are important to consider when the impacts of funding more stringent environmental requirements through water charges are being assessed. Consolidation (at least of payments for environmental improvements) may be important to allow for a better alignment between the costs and benefits of meeting requirements. Flexibility in the delivery of environmental improvements can be particularly important where the efficient plant size is likely to be small. Economies of scale in relation to tertiary treatment provision may make consideration of alternatives ways of improving outcomes (including e.g. those based on enhanced catchment management) particularly important to consider.

Participants indicated the following next steps:

- Further discuss appropriate scales and levels of consolidation with regards to cost recovery and the financing of increasingly stringent environmental policies.

Resources shared by participants

- European Court of Auditors (2021), The Polluter Pays Principle: Inconsistent application across EU environmental, https://www.eca.europa.eu/Lists/ECADocuments/SR21_12/SR_polluter_pays_principle_EN.pdf

References

European Environment Agency (2022), *European Environment Agency, Indicators, Pesticides in rivers, lakes and groundwater*, https://www.eea.europa.eu/ims/pesticides-in-rivers-lakes-and (accessed on 2022). [2]

IEA (2022), *IEA*, https://www.iea.org/data-and-statistics/charts/share-of-russia-in-european-union-and-united-kingdom-gas-demand-2001-2021 (accessed on 2022). [3]

Nödler, K., T. Licha and D. Voutsa (2013), "Twenty years later – Atrazine concentrations in selected coastal waters of the Mediterranean and the Baltic Sea", *Marine Pollution Bulletin*, Vol. 70/1-2, pp. 112-118, https://doi.org/10.1016/j.marpolbul.2013.02.018. [1]

Notes

[1] Data reflects 2016 practices, as captured by a 2017 survey of 338 networks.

2 The implementation of the Polluter Pays Principle

Polluter Pays is a core principle of the WFD. Member states face similar challenges with its implementation, in particular as regards the identification of the polluter and his/her contribution to the pollution into - or the environmental pressure on - the water body. The chapter explores options to implement the principle in the case of diffuse pollution, and clarifies issues in relation to the notion of disproportionate costs. It discusses how the principle is it fit for the new ambition of European policies.

The thematic workshop - part of a series aimed to facilitate the implementation of the economics of the WFD in European Member States - gathered over 100 participants, including government representatives, Directorate Generals (European Commission), utilities and utilities associations, NGOs, and research institutions.

The workshop, co-convened by the OECD and the European Commission - DG ENV, focused on the Polluter Pays Principle. It aimed at:

1. Increasing attention to approaches targeting polluters outside the water and sanitation sectors; raising awareness of water charges inequality across sectors and users;
1. Identifying and disseminating good practices and emerging approaches related to assessing disproportionate costs;
2. Exchanging experiences and knowledge to promote a sustainable, effective and efficient application of the Polluter Pays Principle based on cost recovery assessment;
3. Reflecting on current instruments in place in Member States in relation to the new level of ambition of the European Green Deal.

Speakers with diverse backgrounds shared their experience related to the Polluter Pays Principle and the WFD goals. Highlights of the discussions are provided below. The agenda, a background note and speakers' slides are available on the meeting webpage.

Key messages

Session 1: How the Polluter Pays principle applies for diffuse pollution. The case of agriculture.

- The WFD has translated into a diversity of approaches and policy instruments to address diffuse pollution (Danish pesticide tax, French pesticide and nitrate fee and Dutch phosphate cap). Some instruments may not be fully aligned with the Polluter Pays Principle.
- Currently, there is a disconnection between water sector challenges and their solution in other sectors. Therefore, when addressing diffuse pollution (as well as other water challenges), a wider scale of analysis is required, where interlinkages with other sector, such as climate change mitigation and adaptation and territorial development, need to be considered. Decision makers in the water sector need to understand other sectors' goals and operation dynamics as well as external factors to identify opportunities for addressing water challenges.

Session 2: How the Polluter Pays principle applies for diffuse pollution. Extended producer's responsibility. The case of contaminants of emerging concern.

- A European fund based on contributions from corporates which produce, import or market contaminants of emerging concern (CECs) could be a solution to address diffuse water pollution, under specific conditions. Extended Producer Responsibility (EPR) is most appropriate when it can spur innovation and minimise pollution at source.
- The water sector would benefit from closer collaboration with other sectors such as health and industry to transition from an end-of-pipe approach to a prevention approach for diffuse pollution.
- The geographical scale at which Cost Benefit Analysis are done has implications for the costs and benefits identified. For example, participants indicated the need to consider transboundary issues; think of hydro morphological measures and diffuse pollution.

Session 3: The Polluter Pays principle in relation to disproportionate costs.

- Members States experience similar issues when justifying disproportionate costs, which relate to data, methods and scale. Site specific data is required, which in general is lacking, in particular non-use value, the quantitative impact (benefits) of measures and reference values. Most members States do not have a well-established methodology for assessing disproportionality, therefore there is no clarity on the criteria to use for justification. The geographic and temporal scale selected for carrying out the Cost Benefit Analysis affect the magnitude of disproportionate costs. In addition, the way climate change projections are factored in modify estimation for costs and benefits.
- Several options to justify disproportionate costs were mentioned. The current methodologies, tools and databases need improvement. Mobilising additional sources of funding from other sectors can reduce disproportionately.
- In relation to the next Programme of Measures and disproportionate costs justification, participants indicated several challenges: (1) keeping the motivation required to reach the level of ambition, (2) when increasing monitoring more issues may rise due to having access to updated or new data which was not previously available, therefore more exceptions may be required and (3) Member States have already implemented the most cost effective measures to reduce pollution, therefore the remaining ones may be more costly.
- Participants made it clear that lowering ambitions is not considered an option, as environmental problems will still remain.

Session 4: The Polluter Pays principle and the new Zero Pollution ambition.

- The revised list of surface and groundwater pollutants will be adopted in September 2022. It contains four groups: pesticides, pharmaceuticals, industrial and metals substances. Once the substances are listed, Member States are required to monitor them and reduce their pollution level to specific thresholds.
- Lack of coherence between Directives limits pollution prevention for water bodies. It challenges the ambition of the Zero Pollution Action Plan.
- In relation to circular economy initiatives, the new regulation on minimum requirements for water reuse for irrigation, to be applied by 2023, is expected to stimulate and facilitate water reuse in Member States.

Next steps

Participants indicated as priority the following next steps:

- Sharing drivers and solutions on the best combination of instruments available to address diffuse pollution across policy areas such as agriculture, energy, climate adaptation and mitigation and other sectors, to incentive a change in farmers' practices;
- A dedicated workshop to explore the wider idea of dedicated European funds to cover the pollution costs from the main pollutants and polluting sectors such as pharmaceutical industry and agriculture;
- Common Implementation Strategy (CIS) to explore the geographic and temporal dimension and implication of economic instruments to address pollution. Such an analysis could include the tools used as well the methodologies, for example, Cost Benefit Analysis at transboundary scale;
- A dedicated workshop on the possibility of anchoring the Extended Producer Responsibility (EPR) to the Urban Wastewater Directive, to allow Member States to subsequently implement EPR in national laws;

- A dedicated workshop to exchange experience on dealing with transboundary benefits when assessing disproportionate costs;
- A dedicated workshop on methodologies for assessing impact of measures;
- A dedicated workshop on sharing good practices among Member States on options for circular economy in relation to re-use water.
- CIS to assess the costs of the missed opportunity for water reuse and sludge management due to water pollution.

Session 1: How the Polluter Pays principle applies for diffuse pollution. The case of agriculture

Diffuse pollution is one of the main challenges for reaching the WFD goals by 2027. Despite improvements in water quality, Member States have not reached the required levels. In monitoring sites, pesticides (mainly approved insecticides and herbicides) are present in 13% to 30% of the surface waters, and 3% to 7% of ground waters (mainly atrazine, banned since 2004) (Nödler, Licha and Voutsa, 2013[1]). Since 2010, pesticides concentration is stable in European groundwater and surface water bodies (European Environment Agency, 2022[2]). Phosphate and phosphorus have decreased in waterbodies due to improvements in wastewater treatment and reduction of phosphorus in detergents. However, a slight increase has been observed in the past years (European Environment Agency, 2022[2]).

Diffuse pollution illustrates a deviation from the Polluter Pays Principle application in Member States. The cost of remediation, meaning the cost of treatment necessary to bring abstracted water up to drinking water quality standards, is covered by domestic water users rather than the polluters (or in some cases by irrigators). The WFD has translated into a diversity of approaches and policies instruments to address diffuse pollution (Danish pesticide tax, French pesticide and nitrate fee and Dutch phosphate cap), which in some cases may not be fully aligned with the Polluter Pays Principle, such as payments for ecosystems[1].

The Scottish Environment Protection Agency has developed an approach to tackle diffuse pollution under its first, second and third River Basin Management Plan (RBMP), achieving 87% of water bodies with at least good water quality in 2021. Under this approach, priority catchments were selected, leading to 6 300 initial farm visits. The selection was based on evidences (water quality level, protected areas and designated areas). The buy-in from farmers was obtained through a combination of measures. At national level, legal minimum standards of performance were established, guidance was provided via communication materials and (subsidised) technical advice was available for farmers. At catchment level, experts monitored compliance with environmental regulation through farms visits. The compliance rate rose from 36% to 54% from the first to the second cycle of RBMP. Farmers had 12 months to fix any problem indicated in the evaluation report detailing breaches. The agro-environment climate scheme under the Rural Development programme provided targeted support to help farmers to go beyond the legal minimum. In many cases, the measures to reduce diffuse pollution required only changes in management practices such as livestock management and buffer zones extensions, which do not need major financial investments from farmers. However, it was needed to make the case between the river pollution level and farming practices to ensure buy-in from farmers.

Participants indicated that from a farmer's perspective soil quality is more relevant than water quality. Therefore, when addressing diffuse pollution from farming, the water community would benefit from including soil quality aspects to reach agreement on measures with the agricultural sector and in particular with the farming community.

Due to the complexity of addressing diffuse pollution, transitional measures or instruments are considered by Member States. For example, Payments for Ecosystem Services can be considered a transitional instrument to reduce diffuse pollution in the long term and they can be a cost effective solution in the short term for water suppliers. However, this instrument should be included in a wider territorial strategy to ensure its effectiveness and structural changes, even after its removal. Another strategy can be progressively increasing pollution standards. For example, in some countries, at the beginning of the diffuse pollution strategy, the government paid farmers for measures implemented on top of compliance rules to stimulate higher standards. In a short time period (around 5 years), these higher levels become the new standards and farmers had to comply. Previous support is supposed to enhance the rate of compliance when new standards are put in place.

Equity concerns are a common challenge for Member States when addressing diffuse pollution. They can rise when putting in place economic instruments. For example, fairness issues can appear when adding charges on diffuse pollution to the water bill for irrigators to reduce transaction costs. This may not be aligned with the Polluter Pays Principle because (1) all irrigators are paying the charge regardless of their pollution and (2) other polluters such as livestock farms may not be covering their diffuse pollution costs. However, putting in place a more pragmatic solution (for example diffuse pollution charges for irrigators) can be more cost effective than a more precise charge requiring higher level of baseline data and monitoring. Passing diffuse pollution treatment costs to domestic water users through the water bill can compromise affordability.

During the session, participants indicated that only a few countries have put in place economic instruments to address diffuse pollution. Charges on polluters and taxes on inputs are the most common instruments. In relation to taxing fertilisers, several difficulties were highlighted: (1) imported food may not internalise pollution costs, making EU products less competitive and moving pollution outside of Europe; (2) organic farming can produce diffuse pollution from nutrients and it is not covered under this instrument; (3) fertilisers use is not strictly equivalent to pollution, it depends on farming practices and pedo-climatic factors; and (4) in the short term fertilisers use elasticity is low, farmers need to use a minimum to ensure their production under conventional farming practices. Also, participants indicated that legislation and regulatory instruments are needed in combination with economic instruments to tackle diffuse pollution.

External factors to the water and agricultural sector influence pesticides use and indirectly water quality. For example, increase and volatility in energy prices will impact on synthetic pesticides and fertilizers prices in the near future (as well as food commodities). Similarly, higher environmental expectation from citizens as translated by the Zero Pollution Ambition Plan of the Green Deal may impact positively water bodies' pollution.

Participants indicated that countries are addressing diffuse pollution collectively mainly at catchment level or through food territorial plans and food branding/labels. Labelling requires collaboration between farmers and the administration to provide information to consumers.

Currently, there is a disconnection between water sector challenges and their solution in other sectors. Therefore, when addressing diffuse pollution, a wider scale of analysis is required, where interlinkages with other sectors' objectives such as climate change adaptation and mitigation and territorial development are considered and aligned. Decision makers in the water sector need to understand other sectors' goals and operation as well as external factors affecting them to identify opportunities for addressing water challenges. For example, the additional treatment needed to tackle diffuse pollution produces supplementary greenhouse emissions, which need to be taken into account when putting in place national and regional mitigation strategies.

Participants indicated as priority the following next steps:

- Sharing drivers and solutions on the best combination of instruments available to address diffuse pollution across policy areas such as agriculture, energy, climate adaptation and mitigation and other sectors, to incentive a change in farmers' practices.

Resources shared by participants

- Netherlands, the Task force Agricultural Water Management: https://agrarischwaterbeheer.nl/content/task-force-agricultural-water-management
- EurEau: https://www.eureau.org/documents/drinking-water/briefing-note/4433-briefing-note-on-cooperation-projects-between-water-operators-and-farmers/file
- Netherlands, food chain initiatives for more sustainable dairy production:
- https://www.rijkeweidevogelfonds.nl/
- Netherlands, bringing together the water and agriculture sector: http://www.davidpublisher.com/index.php/Home/Article/index?id=33416.html

Session 2: How the Polluter Pays principle applies for diffuse pollution. Extended producer's responsibility. The case of Contaminants of Emerging Concern

Addressing Contaminants of Emerging Concerns comes at a cost. A relevant question in the context of this thematic workshop relates to the allocation of this cost. Extended Producer Responsibility posits that corporates that put harmful substances on the market should be held accountable for the costs of remediation. In that case, corporates and their customers – not water users – cover the cost of pollution control. Participants highlighted that Extended Producer Responsibility should not be applied for point source pollution, which is best addressed through the Industrial Emission Directive.

In Germany, the problem of trace substances can be reduced to a small number of harmful substances, which come from two main industries, notably agriculture (pesticides – herbicides and insecticides) and the pharmaceutical industry. Based on a case study in North Rhine Westphalia, 14 out of the 20 main substances come from these two industries. The three main substances account for more than 81% of total harm and the 10 main substances for 95%.

The German Association of Energy and Water Industries presented their proposal for a fund for financing the treatment of Contaminants of Emerging Concerns. The fund is based on contributions from manufactures and importers of Contaminants of Emerging Concerns for the entire country. Payments into the fund are calculated according to the relative harmfulness of the trace substances. Based on continuous testing, the payment will be adjusted according to the level of trace substances inputs (and new substances appearance). The fund would be used to cover wastewater treatment companies' expansion required to eliminate trace substances, as well as drinking water suppliers' measures to reduce trace substances. The fund would not prescribe any particular technology; therefore polluters would be free to decide the measures to reduce trace substances pollution.

Participants suggested that this type of fund should be applied at European scale, to cover transboundary implications. In addition, other elements should be explored in relation to the fund: (1) to ensure that importers in the EU market contribute to the fund, and (2) to include contaminant sediments as well as other pollution elements in water. In addition, the following limits were indicated: (1) no environmental standards exist for all substances, (2) how to include new substances into the fund, and (3) how to set the fund contribution to incentivise pollution reduction among polluters.

A French water industry presented experience with Extended Producer Responsibility in France. Wastewater treatment costs are rising due to historical pollution and Contaminants of Emerging Concern. In addition, users have growing health and environmental concerns, which translate in higher expectations for water quality. Some French utilities created an industry-wide coordination group to assess the state of play of the sector, develop new ideas and propose solutions to identified challenges. Three options were identified: (1) to balance the current system to ensure cost recovery and enough funding through economic and regulatory instruments (taxes and Extended Producer Responsibility); (2) to create an international fund for water to cover the costs; and (3) to revisit the current economic model by changing its foundation (indicators and funding mechanism) to reflect the current and future challenges (demography, population density, legacy and new pollution, ecological transition, etc.).

Participants indicated that the water sector needs to collaborate with other sectors such as health (DG SANTE) and industry to be able to move from an end-of-pipe approach to prevention. In addition, participants highlighted that Extended Producer Responsibility should consider the pathway of the pollution, and not only the value chain.

As regards pharmaceutical pollutants, health authorities should be informed of the additional costs paid by water users, as well as the additional costs for society in the long term due to supplementary and cumulative environmental and health issues. Solutions which reduce pollution emitted into water bodies, without compromising the health and treatment results for patients, need collaboration between health authorities, the pharmaceutical industry and the water sector. Education campaigns among medical practitioners and consumers to reduce overconsumption for non-vital medication. Workshop participants mentioned: (1) increasing control on over-the-counter medication, (2) taking into account environmental impacts for non-vital medication approval including monitoring procedure for the substances through the product cycle, (3) current treatment (including wastewater treatment) capacity for the substances, (4) considering contaminants potential cocktail effects and (5) assessing the additional costs required for treatment. However, changing the composition of pharmaceutical products requires several years (more than 6 years on average), from research to market access. It is a similar situation for changing the composition of medication already on the market.

Therefore, a strategy to reduce pollutants into the water should have several components, considering different timescales. In the Netherlands, the introduction of a levy on pharmaceuticals to pay for additional treatment of specific substances has been considered. According to the discussion, charging pollution costs on patients who have to take a particular medicine is not viable from a health perspective, because it encourages them not to use the medicine. In this case, the consumer, meaning the patient, may not be the best entry point for economic instruments due to health and equity concerns. However, the levy should target medicines which have less harmful alternatives. In addition, when considering the levy, it is important to note that most pharmaceutical products are produced outside Europe; this requires measures which can incentivise manufacturers to change the compositions in countries having less stringent regulation.

The discussion highlighted that due consideration should be given to the geographical scale at which Cost Benefit Analysis are performed. Several costs or benefits only materialise at specific geographical scales. For example, participants indicated the need to consider transboundary scale in some instance. This challenge applies to hydro morphological measures as well as diffuse (and point source) pollution. For example, morphological measure for the Haringvliet locks in the Netherlands, which involved opening the lock to allow fish to migrate upstream, would not have been carried out due to its high costs, if only downstream benefits had been taken into account. However, the assessment took into account the benefits upstream as well.

Participants indicated the following next steps as priority:

- Additional research and consultation to explore the opportunity of (a) European fund(s) to cover the pollution costs from the main pollutants and polluting sectors such as pharmaceutical and agriculture. Some participants indicated their interest in exploring the idea of a compulsory financing mechanism for producers of micro pollutants to finance additional waste water treatment capacity. Other participants advocated for compensating sectors affected by pollution (such as those that handle sediments);
- CIS could explore the geographic and temporal dimension and implication of economic instruments to address pollution;

- A dedicated workshop on the possibility of anchoring the Extended Producer Responsibility to the Urban Wastewater Directive, to allow Member States to subsequently implement it in national laws.

Resources shared by participants

- OECD (2019), Pharmaceutical Residues in Freshwater: Hazards and Policy Responses, OECD Studies on Water, OECD Publishing, Paris, https://doi.org/10.1787/c936f42d-en.

Session 3: The Polluter Pays principle in relation to disproportionate costs

Members States share common issues when attempting to justify disproportionate costs. Firstly, justifying disproportionate costs requires to mobilise important human, financial and technical resources. As an illustration, for its second River Basin Management Plan, France had to carry out 710 Cost Benefit Analyses corresponding to waterbodies or group of waterbodies. Secondly, to justify exemptions, site specific data is required, which in general is lacking. In particular, participants highlighted the lack of data in relation to non-use value, the quantitative impact (benefits) of measures and reference values. Thirdly, Members States do not have a well-established methodology for assessing disproportionality, therefore there is no clarity or consistency on the criteria to use for justification.

France has developed a methodology for the economic analysis of disproportionate cost, based on a tool that facilitates the use of economic analysis at sub-sovereign level. Water agencies use it when preparing the Programme of Measures. The tool is a spreadsheet which links environmental measures, their benefits and costs based on reference values. It was updated in 2014. The tool does the calculation based on the water body information inputted (physical data such as water volume and population). Market benefits are estimated based on wastewater treatment costs saved and non-market benefits are based on population density and population willingness to pay for recreational activities or interest in natural heritage. A 20% error margin is applied based on the assumptions that costs are overestimated and benefits are underestimated. Several difficulties were reported when using the tool: (1) choosing the relevant population to which the benefit unit is applied and (2) accounting for non-quantifiable benefits. Currently, the tool is being updated for the fourth River Basin Management Plans by a group of practitioners and environmental economists. The main goals are to update values for existing benefits and new monetised benefits, make the assessment more robust, and make the tool more user friendly.

The Netherlands indicated that implementing all measures and achieving all objectives in one cycle would be practically impossible due to lack of staff, and to disproportionate cost and affordability issues: a 30% to 40% increase in levies would be required to cover the costs of measures. A less brutal – and more socially acceptable – increase would suffice, if additional delays were provided to achieve WFD objectives. For the third Programme of Measures, EUR 1 500 million will be disbursed between 2021 and 2027 on top of the measures under the Urban Waste Water Treatment Directive and Nitrate Directive. Discussions with the agriculture sector are exploring measures to avoid disproportionate costs. Subsidies to farmers have been identified as a potential source of funding; however only 10% of the measures are eligible. Measures will increase 2.4% on average costs (up to 17% for arable farming) for farmers, further affecting farmers' revenues.

Progress has been made in relation to the ecological status. However, it is not reflected in official data, because of the "one out – all out" rule. It was suggested that exemptions could be attributed per substances instead of per water body, which would increase the number of water bodies in good status.

Several solutions to address disproportionate costs were mentioned. Most of all, pollution prevention and avoidance are the best strategy to reduce disproportionate costs in the future. Mobilising additional sources of funding from other sectors can reduce disproportionality, for example subsidies and eco-schemes from the new Common Agriculture Policy. However, careful design of financial support is required to align with the Polluter Pays Principle, if public budgets, including EU funds – and not polluters - are used for remediation activities.

Participants highlighted the difficulty to bring additional sources of funding from other sectors due to misaligned sectoral objectives and trade-offs. Agriculture is a case in point. Further, the discussion highlighted the need to link measures required to reach good status with political agendas such as climate change, to increase opportunities for funding and action.

In relation to the next Programme of Measures, participants indicated the difficulty to keep the motivation required to comply with the WFD. Monitoring capacities improves, more issues may rise due to updated or new data; therefore more exemptions may be required. In addition, Member States have already implemented the most cost effective measures to reduce pollution, therefore pending challenges are likely to be more costly.

Participants suggested the following next steps:

- Further exchange of experience on dealing with transboundary benefits when assessing disproportionate costs;
- A dedicated workshop on methodologies for assessing the impact of measures.

Resources shared by participants

- France, Tool guidance document http://temis.documentation.developpement-durable.gouv.fr/document.html?id=Temis-0080405
- European Court of Auditors, The Polluter Pays Principle: Inconsistent application across EU environmental policies and actions https://www.eca.europa.eu/en/Pages/DocItem.aspx?did=58811
- Taskforce on Agricultural Management, https://agrarischwaterbeheer.nl/content/task-force-agricultural-water-management

Session 4: The Polluter Pays principle and the new Zero Pollution ambition

The Zero Pollution Action Plan includes targets to achieve the objectives within the different EU laws (related to air, water, marine and others). A revised list of surface and groundwater pollutants will be adopted in September 2022. It contains four groups: pesticides, pharmaceuticals, industrial and metals substances. Once the substances are listed, Member States are required to monitor them and reduce their presence to the specific thresholds. The Commission is not planning to set rules and guidelines to identify the polluters of each substance.

Lack of coherence between Directives limits pollution prevention for waterbodies, and consequently, may affect the achievement of the Zero Pollution ambition. For instance, participants pointed out the discrepancy between Registration, Evaluation, Authorisation and Restriction of Chemical (REACH) EU Regulation and the WFD objectives. Under the REACH regulation, substances' toxicity needs to be proven before use can be limited or banned; therefore remediation will be required ex post to remove pollution from water bodies.

The Zero Pollution Action Plan emphasises the circular economy. Three sets of initiatives were mentioned, which align with WFD ambition. First, Cyprus[2] and the south of Spain (Murcia) were identified as models of wastewater reuse, in particular for agriculture. The new Regulation on minimum requirement for water reuse for irrigation, to be applied by 2023, is expected to stimulate and facilitate water reuse in Member States. Second, Ireland is upgrading the first facility to recover phosphorous from wastewater, as part of the Ringsend Wastewater Treatment Plant Upgrade Project, treating approximately 40% of the total public

Irish wastewater. The project aims to sustainably treat wastewater for 2.4 million p.e. while achieving the standards of the Urban Wastewater Treatment Directive. The agricultural sector is the target for the phosphorous recovered from the treatment. Third, in the navigation sector, initiatives exist for reusing sediments removed from water bodies to maintain safe navigation. The sediments are re-used in several production processes like construction. Participants highlighted the need to ensure consistency between the definition of pollution in the WFD and the Zero Pollution Action Plan as well as the alignment of the Waste Directive and the possibility of using products from waste water treatment.

Participants suggested the following next steps:

- Sharing good practices among Member States as regards water re-use;
- CIS to assess missed opportunities for circular economy due to water pollution (water reuse and sludge management).

Resources shared by participants

- Netherlands, projects working on circular agricultural economy: https://www.vruchtbarekringloop.nl/
- Ireland, the Phosphorous recovery project information, https://www.water.ie/news/works-progress-on-the-rin/
- Netherlands, recovery of substances from wastewater projects: https://www.kwrwater.nl/en/onderzoek/sustainability-water-cycle-en/sustainable-resources/
- E-flow management and wastewater, Dinar, A., & Tsur, Y. (2021). The Economics of Water Resources: A Comprehensive Approach. Cambridge: Cambridge University Press. doi:10.1017/9781316678640
- Circular economy for water: https://www.eureau.org/documents/waste-water/briefing-note-1/3010-briefing-note-on-water-and-the-circular-economy-package/file
- Sediment management examples of circular economy and NBS, https://sednet.org/workshop-navclimate-sednet-10-11-feb-2021-2/ Other examples can be accessed via the SedNet website www.sednet.org

References

European Environment Agency (2022), *European Environment Agency, Indicators, Pesticides in rivers, lakes and groundwater*, https://www.eea.europa.eu/ims/pesticides-in-rivers-lakes-and (accessed on 2022). [2]

IEA (2022), *IEA*, https://www.iea.org/data-and-statistics/charts/share-of-russia-in-european-union-and-united-kingdom-gas-demand-2001-2021 (accessed on 2022). [3]

Nödler, K., T. Licha and D. Voutsa (2013), "Twenty years later – Atrazine concentrations in selected coastal waters of the Mediterranean and the Baltic Sea", *Marine Pollution Bulletin*, Vol. 70/1-2, pp. 112-118, https://doi.org/10.1016/j.marpolbul.2013.02.018. [1]

Notes

[1] PES are fully aligned with the PPP when *additional* eco-system services are clearly defined and monitored.

[2] Note by Turkey: The information in this document with reference to "Cyprus" relates to the southern part of the Island. There is no single authority representing both Turkish and Greek Cypriot people on the Island. Turkey recognises the Turkish Republic of Northern Cyprus (TRNC). Until a lasting and equitable solution is found within the context of the United Nations, Turkey shall preserve its position concerning the "Cyprus issue".

Note by all the European Union Member States of the OECD and the European Union: The Republic of Cyprus is recognised by all members of the United Nations with the exception of Turkey. The information in this document relates to the area under the effective control of the Government of the Republic of Cyprus.

3 Water scarcity

Water scarcity has recently emerged as a pan-European challenge. In that context, participants in the thematic workshop revived discussions on the practical modalities of water allocation regimes in relation to achieving the objectives of the Water Framework Directive, in combination with pricing mechanisms. Options to bolster diffusion of nature-based solutions and reclaimed water were discussed. The chapter explains the complex dynamics of water use efficiency as a response to water scarcity.

The thematic workshop – part of a series aimed to facilitate the implementation of the economics of the WFD in European Member States - gathered some 90 participants, including government representatives, Directorate Generals (European Commission), utilities and utilities associations, NGOs, and research institutions.

The workshop, co-convened by the OECD and the European Commission - DG ENV, focused on the economics of water scarcity. The following topics were discussed in three interrelated sessions:

- Allocation regimes, in the context of the WFD: definition of return and e-flows, reflecting flexibility in water entitlements, water allocation reforms, relationship with pricing;
- Incentives to increase demand for reclaimed water;
- Scaling up nature-based solutions (NbS) to enhance water retention.

Speakers with diverse backgrounds shared their experience related to the economics of water scarcity and the WFD goals. Highlights of the discussions are provided below. The agenda, a background note and speakers' slides are available on the meeting webpage.

Key messages

Session 1: Water allocation regimes, in the context of the WFD

- Water allocation regimes are an integral part of measures to achieve the ambition of the WFD. In particular, ecological and return flows should be factored in. Prevailing regimes tend to disregard new users and the navigation sector.
- Water use efficiency can have detrimental effects on water availability and quality, if not accompanied by robust water allocation regimes that determine how to use the water saved through efficiency measures.
- Further work in the context of the WFD would require participation of other sectors (agriculture, energy, fluvial transportation…).

Session 2: Incentives to increase demand for reclaimed water

- The main incentive in place in EU member states is a low price for reclaimed water. Other possible incentives (such as reliability of water supply) do not seem to be considered.
- Reclaimed water requires that water utilities reinvent their business model.
- It is not clear how costs should be shared between different stakeholders. Experience varies across member states.

Session 3: Scaling up nature-based solutions to enhance water retention

- While nature-based solutions for water retention have distinctive advantages, rolling them out at scale faces several practical issues related to lack of data (on costs), challenges to value multiple co-benefits, complex institutional arrangements that blur decision-making and accountability.
- A pending issue of whether and how economic policy instruments can support their deployment at scale.
- Professional education is required so that more engineers are aware and competent for the design and operation of NbS.

Next steps

Participants indicated as priority the following next steps:

- The European Commission to set up an *ad hoc* Task Group on water allocation regimes, with a view to facilitate experience sharing across member states. The Task Group should bring in sectors that use water (agriculture, energy, fluvial transportation…).
- Member states would benefit from further guidance on how to price and finance the production and distribution of reclaimed water. In particular, further analysis on whether – or under which conditions – subsidies can be economically beneficial would be valuable.

Several options were suggested that may accelerate the deployment of nature-based solutions for water retention, where appropriate:

- Clarify how the soon-to-be-released regulation on Nature Restoration can be oriented to favour NbS;
- Institutional arrangements and regulation to better combine soil and water management;
- Document the economic value NbS generate;
- Explore how the taxonomy on sustainable activities provides incentives to direct commercial finance towards NbS;
- Set up a helpdesk to support project development and project owners;
- Review experience with de-sealing sealed surfaces.

Session 1: Water allocation regimes, in the context of the WFD

Over-abstraction is a major problem in the European Union. It derives from a combination of increasing water demand (for urban water supply, agriculture, and other economic activities) and variability of precipitations (both magnified by climate change). Water scarcity triggers justice issues. Exposure and vulnerability to scarcity are heterogeneous among water users and income level. It follows that managing water scarcity is gaining traction as a condition for good status of water bodies and a requisite to deliver on multiple EU strategies (including the EU biodiversity strategy).

Banning specific water uses can only be a short-term response to water scarcity. It fails to reflect the distinctive capacities of different water users to adjust to scarcity. It does not contribute to long term flexibility of water management. When banning is considered as part of a menu of options to address scarcity crises, the protocol needs to be set before the drought occurs.

Water allocation regimes contribute to the objectives of the WFD, as regards quantitative status of groundwater and quantitative management of all freshwater sources. They are particularly relevant where water is scarce and competition to use available sources intensifies. Well-designed water allocation regimes can reach economic efficiency, environmental sustainability and social equity. They promote efficiency and reduce waste. They send signals where to invest, such as to increase water storage and water efficiency.

Robust water allocation regimes are based on comprehensive data sets:

- A water balance, to define and monitor resource availability and use. Countries reported cases where fragmented institutional frameworks lead to lack of cohesive view of the water balance;
- A definition of the abstractable pool and the capacity to monitor legal and illegal abstraction;
- Reference flows. They send a signal about security of supply;

- Ecological flows. They determine how much water is required to sustain ecosystems and the services they deliver.

Progress is made, as new sources of data become available. Several countries shared experience with the use of new sources of data (typically Copernicus) to monitor water abstraction, or soil moisture).

In practice, water allocation regimes in Europe still face several pending issues:

- Compliance. Participants at the workshop reported basins where caps on abstractable water are not properly enforced and complied with;
- Environmental flows. In the context of the Common Implementation Strategy, material was developed to guide decisions regarding ecological flows. Little progress has been reported, though, on the definition of e-flows and compliance with set levels. Uncertainty remains on whether e-flows are best defined as an absolute volume of water (number of m^3 required to support ecosystems) or a share of available water (at the risk of affecting the integrity of ecosystems in times of low flows);
- Equity issues. They are particularly acute where allocation regimes fail to account for the need of selected users (e.g. fluvial transportation) or disregard new users (new entrants in a river basin);
- Balance. A balance needs to be found between securing access to water (in particular for high-value uses) and the ability to adjust to shifting circumstances. Robust water allocation regimes deliver in times of plenty and in times of scarcity;
- Transaction costs. Minimal transaction costs are a condition for effective water allocation regimes. They are a distinctive strength of tradable water entitlements in the Murray Darling basin (Australia), where water can be traded via a mobile app.

Box 3.1. Australia - Water Market Reform – case study input

Waterflow is a mobile app designed for use by water market participants, who are primarily rural irrigators, in the Murray Darling Basin. While users can't trade directly on the app, the app facilitates price discovery, allows users to search for water to buy and provides trade information (including how to make a trade and associated transaction costs).

Waterflow resulted from an Australian Government funded Business Research Innovation Initiative targeting small to medium business to come up with innovative solutions to priority challenges for government.

Improving the quality and transparency of water markets information was identified as one of the priority challenges. The dominant issue has been price discovery resulting from:

- Dispersed information sources including separate Australian Basin State water trade registers and several separate water exchanges, requiring market participants to know of and go to numerous sources to aid price discovery;
- Time lags between actual trades and their recording on Australian Basin State registers limiting the transparency of "today's" market;
- Inaccurate price reporting including many zero-dollar trades;
- Incomplete register information where the purpose of the trade isn't captured meaning spots, forwards, and leases cannot be separated.

The app pulls water market information from numerous information sources and provides users access to market information wherever they have mobile phone access. This is particularly important for users with poor internet access due to poor connectivity or because they are working away from a computer.

The app reduces information asymmetry and increases market participant confidence to trade. In addition to this app, work by Basin Governments is ongoing to improve the confidence and integrity of water markets. The Australian Government has recently announced its commitment to reforms to:

- Introduce integrity safeguards to water markets, including applying professional standards to intermediaries comparable with other markets;
- Ensure water market participants have sufficient information to make informed water trading decisions; and
- Improve the functioning, transparency, and governance of water markets.

Under these reforms, the Bureau of Meteorology will design new data standards and a new national water data hub and water market website. These platforms will automatically capture, transfer, and publish existing and new data to improve transparency and inform trade-related decisions in water markets.

Groundwater allocation triggers distinctive challenges, for several reasons. First, data on groundwater availability is patchy. Second, monitoring groundwater abstraction and use can be difficult. Unregulated water use is reported in many water basins in Europe.

It is noteworthy that security comes at a cost: higher security in water supply requires access to more expensive resources (storage, or desalination, for instance). The appropriate level of water security ultimately is a political decision, which reflects how much a community is willing to pay for it.

An interesting topic is the interplay between water allocation regimes and pricing mechanisms (here, essentially abstraction charges). According to economic theory, abstraction charges reflect the opportunity cost of using water. They are meant to increase when water is scarce (assuming demand is constant).

Also, increased uncertainty about water availability now and in the future enhances the need for a buffer stock of water, to be used in times of scarcity. Viable cost recovery requires that a "scarcity premium" applies to access that water.

Measures to enhance water use efficiency can trigger a rebound effect, where water saved through efficiency gains is used for other purposes (such as extension of irrigated land, or growing more water-intensive crops). Water allocation regimes are instrumental in addressing this rebound effect. This requires that return flows (or net abstraction) are considered and measured.

Resources shared by participants

- A note on how to tackle illegal water abstraction: https://www.fundacionbotin.org/89dguuytdfr276ed_uploads/Observatorio%20Tendencias/How%20to...ok_enlaces.pdf
- An academic paper on remote sensing-based irrigation water accounting at river basin scale https://www.researchgate.net/publication/344427501_Evaluation_of_Remote_Sensing-Based_Irrigation_Water_Accounting_at_River_Basin_District_Management_Scale
- DIANA project on monitoring non-authorised water abstractions for irrigation: https://diana-h2020.eu/en/index.html
- The OECD Health Check for water allocation regimes (https://issuu.com/oecd.publishing/docs/water-resources-allocation-2015-pol). A companion report on groundwater allocation (https://www.oecd.org/environment/groundwater-allocation-9789264281554-en.htm)

Session 2: Incentives to increase demand for reclaimed water

The session was based on the assumption that technologies are available to treat wastewater at the preferred level of quality before it can be reused. So, the question is: how to stimulate demand for reclaimed water? International experience shows a combination of three instruments works best: quality standards, prices, secured volume of reclaimed water. The discussion highlighted that in Europe the first two prevail, while the third one is hardly considered.

Several countries are gaining experience with reclaimed water in Europe, most notably small islands in the Mediterranean region. Investment is driven by lack of freshwater availability. Similarly, some utilities add the provision of reclaimed water as a feature of their business model (beyond water supply, wastewater collection and treatment)[1].

These countries had to overcome initial users' reluctance to use reclaimed water, or crops irrigated with reclaimed water. They testify that communication is key to build trust in the quality of the source and the fact that it is fit for certain purposes. Communication needs to be backed by compliance monitoring and enforcement.

Quality standards are being developed, for instance for agriculture use of reclaimed water. Micropollutants found in wastewater streams attract a lot of attention. This can be an issue for food crops; in some jurisdictions, reclaimed water is allowed for trees and vegetables, but not for vegetables that are consumed raw. It is noteworthy that in the context of the Zero Emission policy, the precautionary principle may make the use of reclaimed problematic.

Where demand for reclaimed water is low, treated effluents can be used to maintain environmental flows in times of scarcity (typically in the summer). It can also be used to recharge aquifers, thus benefitting the status of groundwater bodies. Such opportunities actually derive from the WFD: at European level, the Water Reuse Regulation's provisions on risk management require to take into account possible impact on the environment and call for taking in account EU legislation, including in particular respecting the WFD provisions, thus including ecological flow considerations.

Countries are puzzled as regards the right way to charge users for the use of reclaimed water. The prevailing model seems to be the provision of reclaimed water as a distinctively low price, so that it is more attractive than freshwater. In some countries, users only pay the distribution cost of reclaimed water (not the treatment cost). Such a policy is at odds with the need to recover cost of the provision of reclaimed water. It is also inconsistent with the ambition to promote water use efficiency to discourage wastage. It does not contribute to allocating water where it creates most value.

Pending issues in relation to the business model for reclaimed water include:

- How to reflect environmental and resource costs (or benefits) of reclaimed water?
- Can some sort of payment for ecosystem services apply? The option may be valid when reclaimed water explicitly substitutes for the use of groundwater, or scarce freshwater, which can then remain in the environment and support ecosystems;
- Who should pay the additional treatment required to make reclaimed water fit for purpose? Some member states reported government subsidies to cover the cost of tertiary treatment. It remains to be seen whether and under what conditions such subsidies can be economically effective: subsidising the construction cost can attract more users via network externality; subsidising the input (supplied wastewater) can augment the volume of reclaimed water, further addressing water scarcity.

Reclaimed water is more competitive when abstraction charges for freshwater reflect the opportunity cost of using water (through a scarcity premium or similar mechanism). But this is not common practice in Europe.

Resources shared by participants

- Some success cases of wastewater reuse can be found in the EU project: https://suwanu-europe.eu/

Session 3: Scaling up nature-based solutions to enhance water retention

Natural water retention measures are pervasive in several countries. They apply to both flood prevention (e.g. the Room for the River programme in the Netherlands) and mitigation of water scarcity risks (e.g. aquifer recharge to augment supply, or mulching to manage water demand). Pilot projects illustrate that NbS are valuable and appropriate options, which can deliver multiple co-benefits. However, NbS for water retention are not scaling up in Europe.

Some participants contended that cost-benefit analysis can contribute to scaling up NbS. However, traditional CBAs fail to capture the multiple co-benefits triggered by NbS at the appropriate time scale (long term). Methods and data would need to improve. As regards costs, despite their existing track record, data on the capital and operation and maintenance costs of NbS is lacking. Even if NbS are more expensive than grey solutions, NbS for water retention provide a wide range of co-benefits: these include resilience, cooling effect in urban environments, mental health and many others. In parallel, a thorough assessment of the environmental and social footprint of grey infrastructures (including CO_2 emissions, as documented by Deltares) would help make NbS attractive.

Planning has a role to play. From that perspective, it is unclear whether the WFD – which relies on 5-years cycles – promotes or deters NbS for water management: short timelines imposed by regulation to deliver environmental benefits favour grey infrastructures. The co-benefits of NbS can best be captured when planning cuts across sectors: a narrow focus on water retention fails to capture co-benefits, therefore limiting the comparative advantage of NbS. Water agencies will monitor the contribution of NbS to water retention, but co-benefits are likely to remain unnoticed or unreported. Appropriate planning for NbS combines water, soil, sediments, and biodiversity. Participants also discussed the appropriate geographical scale for planning: landscape approaches provide a wider vision that helps to combine multiple perspectives.

In addition, regulation is required. Member states are at diverse stages in the development of policy and regulation for nature-based solutions for water retention. To be considered in practice, NbS can be integrated to regulation, construction, urban planning, and procurement codes. Land management has a lot to do with NbS for mitigation of flood and scarcity risks.

In Europe, a new policy landscape – including the EU taxonomy for sustainable activities – provides opportunities to consider and finance NbS for water resources management. As financial institutions look for opportunities to increase their funding for resilient projects and infrastructures, the taxonomy can direct more finance towards NbS. It is not clear however whether this will materialise at scale.

A distinctive challenge noted by participants is that NbS are often local. They apply in specific contexts. For instance, distinctive soil structure is required for the sponge function to materialise.

Institutional arrangements are critical. To design and implement NbS, water authorities or other public institutions engage with diverse groups of stakeholders: landowners, farmers, water utilities. Financial incentives may not be the only option, but they do help for several reasons: adjusting existing practices and infrastructure can be costly; and NbS include some risks, which need to be compensated. Because such complex and long-lasting engagement is required, ownership of the solution is blurred: it is not clear who will initiate the collaboration and who will be accountable over time.

A pending issue is whether and how economic policy instruments can incentivise the use of NbS for water retention. For instance, while utilities can pay for groundwater recharge or catchment protection that benefit their operation, it is not clear who can pay for larger-scale programmes. How can landowners be incentivised to accept nature-based water retention measures, which imply wet soils near natural streams? Are taxes on sealed surfaces in urban environment being considered / deployed[2]? Policy reforms and redirection of agriculture subsidies have a role to play.

Resources shared by participants

- The experience of IUCN (https://www.iucn.org/theme/nature-based-solutions/resources/iucn-global-standard-nbs)
- In the Netherlands the Room for the River-programme applied NbS at large scale. The programme ran over more than 10 years and stayed within projected cost and was delivered in time. (https://www.rijkswaterstaat.nl/en/water/water-safety/room-for-the-rivers)
- The MERLIN project, financed by the European Commission under Horizon 2020, commits to transformative ecosystem restoration, mainstreaming nature-based solutions for the urgent systemic change of our society (https://project-merlin.eu/)
- The IMPETUS project, a Horizon 2020 project funded by the European Commission, is an innovative project with the aim of enhancing the resilience of cities in the face of security threats in public spaces (https://www.impetus-project.eu).

References

European Environment Agency (2022), *European Environment Agency, Indicators, Pesticides in rivers, lakes and groundwater*, https://www.eea.europa.eu/ims/pesticides-in-rivers-lakes-and (accessed on 2022). [2]

IEA (2022), *IEA*, https://www.iea.org/data-and-statistics/charts/share-of-russia-in-european-union-and-united-kingdom-gas-demand-2001-2021 (accessed on 2022). [3]

Nödler, K., T. Licha and D. Voutsa (2013), "Twenty years later – Atrazine concentrations in selected coastal waters of the Mediterranean and the Baltic Sea", *Marine Pollution Bulletin*, Vol. 70/1-2, pp. 112-118, https://doi.org/10.1016/j.marpolbul.2013.02.018. [1]

Notes

[1] Interestingly, in countries where water supply service providers are distinct from sanitation service providers, reclaimed water induces competition between these two groups.

[2] France and Germany were mentioned, along cities in the Netherlands (Amsterdam), Wallonia (Jette) and the USA (e.g. Columbia, Philadelphia, Portland).

4 Water investment planning and financing

Better planning can go a long way in facilitating cost-effective compliance with the objectives of the Water Framework and Flood directives. Participants in the thematic workshop explored practical options for planning under uncertainty and sequencing pro projects to raise value created by water-related investments.

Financing programmes of measures and water-related investment remains a key concern for member states. Discussions explored potential new sources of finance for water-related investments, such as land-value capture, depreciation methods for water infrastructures, and extended producers' responsibility.

This thematic workshop is part of a series aimed to facilitate the implementation of the economics of the WFD in European Member States. It was co-convened by the European Commission and the OECD and focussed on topics that can support decisions about water investment planning and financing.

In three distinct sessions, it discussed the following topics:

- Investment planning for uncertainty, particularly related to climate change;
- From investing in projects to investment pathways and the use of analytical frameworks; and
- Harnessing multiple sources of commercial finance.

It addressed challenges faced by Member States and provided a platform to share best practices. Highlights of the discussions are provided below. The agenda, a background note and speakers' slides are available on the meeting webpage.

Key messages

Session 1: Investment planning for uncertainty, particularly related to climate change

- Member States are already integrating climate change in their RBM planning processes and are increasingly making use of multi-criteria analysis and scenario approaches.
- They would benefit from further guidance on methodologies for scenario analysis related to uncertain future climate conditions and on how to reflect impacts and benefits from 'external' actors (notably other sectors and other spatial areas, e.g. transboundary settings). A better use of existing and new data on climate impacts on the local scale could be further integrated in Member States' planning processes.
- Better communication of risks and uncertainties to policy makers, as well as capacity building to support the use of new tools and analyses would be beneficial.

Session 2: From investing in projects to investment pathways

- Strategically sequencing projects can help build resilience and create synergies between individual interventions. A more strategic approach could support Member States to select appropriate measures to meet several objectives simultaneously and to assess and manage trade-offs over longer timeframes.
- Some countries are already using investment pathways and specific tools to account for synergies across measures along different time scales and uncertainty. Further research and guidance on such tools and frameworks would be valuable. Applying complex analysis also requires increased efforts and capacity building to achieve stakeholder engagement.

Session 3: Harnessing multiple sources of private finance

- Member States voiced interest in nature-based solutions (NbS) for water security. A number of successful financing examples of multi stakeholder arrangement for NbS exist. Conducive regulatory frameworks, better coordination across stakeholders and further methods and data can support the valorisation of benefits from water-related projects and support a funding stream.
- Strategic risk sharing arrangements as well as proven compliance with additional policy objectives (e.g., climate objectives) can help attract private finance and new types of investors (e.g. climate/ sustainable finance).

Session 1: Investment planning for uncertainty, particularly related to climate change

Climate change has significant effects on water security and brings high levels of uncertainty related to its impacts on water bodies on a local level and over different time scales. Water management can mitigate these effects. Hence, decision-making tools and flexible, resilience-based planning approaches are vital to ensure that the measures of the river basin management plans (RBMP) are robust, given the climatic, as well as environmental and societal conditions in the near and further future.

Experiences and best practices in Member States

Many European Member states incorporate climate change in their water management planning and most countries refer to the CIS Guidance Document No. 24. A new legislation in Spain, for example, corroborates the interlinkages between national adaptation strategies and water management planning and requires more detailed climate change studies for the RBMPs. Through diversified water supply sources, particularly in the Spanish Mediterranean region, they strengthen resilience for varying levels of water availability. Similarly, Spain has a specific licencing system in place that provides 'ad hoc' water rights, dependent on water availability. This allocation arrangement creates flexibility for the water system for varying levels of water supply and according to seasonal changes.

In Ireland, the national adaptation strategy requires a specific climate adaptation plan for water services and water quality since 2019. Further, RBMPs are circled back and inform national adaptation plans.

The Netherlands deploy a scenario planning approach for water and flood management under the Delta programme and the associated Delta fund. This approach requires selecting measures that are sufficient in each of the elaborate scenarios. The level of ambition for flood protection is determined in terms of a national standard of individual fatality due to flooding of 1 in 100 000 per annum. Further, the prioritisation and decision on individual projects are based on the principal of technical urgency[1] (for more information, see link in 'Resources'). The programme and schedule of measures are re-evaluated and adjusted each year, which allows for an 'on-rolling' and adaptive programme. Measures might include land reservation for possible future flood defence interventions. The latter is a complex political decision, which requires trade-offs between land use and flood defence as well as compensation of land owners.

Overall, Member states deploy a wide array of tools to assess and prioritise the measures under their RBMP. Some countries combine cost-benefit analysis (CBA) with multi-criteria analysis (MCA) (e.g., Bulgaria, Finland, Ireland or Romania). Increasingly, Member States are exploring new tools to account for raising uncertainty, including related to risks of extreme events and to account for longer time horizons. For example, Ireland is exploring alternative tools that reflect risk opportunity analysis. The Netherlands consider combining a risk-orientated approach with stress testing at interregional levels.

Challenges and next steps

During the session, participants voiced the **need for further guidance on such tools and scenario approaches**. More explicit support on methodologies for scenario planning would be required, particularly on planning approaches that incorporate longer planning horizons. Specific guidance could be sued on which types of scenarios can be used, how reference conditions can be determined, how impacts can be measured and how the sensitivity of the scenarios can be tested.

Additionally, participants raised the **need for available climate change data** on the local level and the access to water data. There is room to better identify and mainstream the use of existing climate modelling tools (e.g., Copernicus) for robust water management. Further, digital technologies could help improve water databases.

Further, participants highlighted the challenges around **how to integrate impacts caused by other actors** in their planning approaches, including in transboundary, as well as cross-sectoral contexts. Currently, the attention is given to pressures and states, while there is a lack of comprehensive assessment on drivers and impacts. Similarly, a **better integration of co-benefits** among different actors and sectors would be needed for robust planning and prioritisation processes. Difficulties exist when it comes to justifying expenditures for measures which deliver benefits elsewhere (for example in another country, or for another sector or policy domain). The assessment and selection of sustainable measures would benefit from better and more strategic integration of different sectors, including agriculture, energy, urban planning and navigation at early stages.

A last point raised during the session was the challenge of **effective communication on uncertainties and risks to policy makers**. Similarly, while CBA might not be the appropriate tool for decision-making under uncertainty, policy makers are familiar with it. Participants mentioned that **introducing new tools or concepts raises difficulties**. These insights highlight the importance of explicit guidelines on appropriate tools and approaches to allow their mainstreaming, as well as the need for capacity building or awareness raising among policy makers, water managers and project developers.

Resources shared by participants:

- Information on the Dutch Delta Programme https://englich.deltaprogramma.nl
- Information on Dutch Delta scenarios and adaptive delta management Delta scenarios and adaptive Delta Management | STOWA
- Dutch portal for flood safety program https://waterveiligheidsportaal.nl
- "If you click on "Landelijk veiligheidsbeeld" ("national safety overview") you can see the standards for each part of the dyke, if it is judged against that standard (and if so; you can see the results and download the report that belongs with it) and the reinforcement program for the next years. Water authorities communicate with the national coordinating flood safety program using that portal, so the information is as real time as we can get it."
- Dutch report 'Exploring the costs and benefits of the WFD' (on how benefits are expressed in qualitative terms and in descriptive texts and illustrations by expressing them in terms of ecosystem services)
- https://www.tweedekamer.nl/kamerstukken/detail?id=2021D43941&did=2021D43941 *(available only in Dutch)*
- Information on the Taskforce Agricultural Water Management which establishes cooperation between agricultural entrepreneurs, public bodies and water managers https://agrarischwaterbeheer.nl/content/task-force-agricultural-water-management
- United Nations Economic Commission for Europe (UNECE) Handbook on Water allocation in a transboundary context https://unece.org/environment-policy/publications/handbook-water-allocation-transboundary-context

Session 2: From investing in projects to Strategic Investment Pathways

Water systems are complex and interconnected systems across various spatial and temporal scales and with interdependencies among different users. Water management interventions hence have impacts on a variety of users and across different time horizons, potentially creating externalities and co-benefits. Therefore, water-related projects should be considered as elements of a sequence of strategically linked interventions. Such strategic investment pathways need to be flexible to deal with prevailing and increasing uncertainties and adapt to new conditions as they develop.

Country examples and best practices

Professors Boltz and Brown presented an analytical framework for the design of strategic investment pathways (SIPs) and application in various contexts. The framework deploys existing planning and analysis tools in a systemic approach to ensure optimal investment planning and sequencing of projects to capture synergies across investment value chains. In the first step of the framework, the analyst defines the system's scope as well as the performance objectives and key uncertainties to be addressed. In a European context, such objectives could be defined by the WFD.

The framework's next steps consist of option analyses, under which different possible measures are stress tested for a variety of possible features (scenarios) and in connection with possible follow-on measures. This analysis does not only take into account the short term effects of a measure but also its effect on follow-on investments and on the water system in the future. In Mexico City, this analysis identified that measures to connect existing reservoirs as well as policies to foster cooperation, increase efficiency and to increase rainwater harvesting are the optimal solutions for the problem set. It found that 'transformation[2]' in water management is the key element to achieve the objective of increased and stable water supply. Such a strategic analysis could also support the needed transformation in European country contexts, for example in Spain, which will face increasing pressures due to flood and drought events.

Similar pathway methods are deployed in the Netherlands, where real option analysis is used for flood protection to assess the significance of an investment over longer time horizons (e.g., longer than 35 years) (see link under 'Resources'). Further, Deltares uses adaptation pathways to assess the climate change robustness of interventions over long time horizons. For example, this method allows to anticipate interventions that might be necessary in the future (e.g., land conversion for flood defence), and hence prevents measures that might preclude those interventions. This rationale allows to create synergies between measures that are taken now and measures that are likely to be taken in the future.

Challenges and next steps

In the European context, participants voiced that currently used planning schemes are robust to solve one problem/ achieve one single objective but fail when attempting to combine and achieve several objectives simultaneously. This, however, would be key to ensure the optimal choice of measures when addressing the various objectives under the WFD, as well the challenges related to climate change and other societal and policy objectives. The SIPs framework includes a multi-objective optimisation by design and allows identifying optimal measures according to select priorities among economic, societal and environmental objectives. The integrated multi-criteria analysis allows to visualise and manage arising trade-offs, while taking future constraints and development into the consideration.

While the presented framework can offer valuable methods in theory, its contextualisation in Europe could be challenging and might require further research. Distinctive WFD objectives, e.g., good ecological status and objectives under other directives, e.g. linked to energy efficiency and resilience are more complex to grasp and assess. Overall, the session highlighted the **need for further research and guidance on appropriate tools and methods** to evaluate and chose individual projects as part of strategic pathways.

Another challenge raised by Member States was **limited capacity of local stakeholders and water authorities to conduct complex analysis** (- while the use of CBA seems to be mainstreamed, already MCA has been difficult to implement in some contexts). Experiences from Mexico city and Deltare's work have shown that strong engagement with relevant stakeholders is needed to launch complex analyses and attract participation in these endeavours. Additionally, a stepwise approach, starting with easiest pathways without a full optimisation process could be appropriate.

Resources shared by participants:

- Paper on 'Investment under non-stationarity: economic evaluation of adaptation pathways' https://link.springer.com/article/10.1007/s10584-019-02409-6
- Paper on 'Benefits and Limitations of Real Options Analysis for the Practice of River Flood Risk Management' https://agupubs.onlinelibrary.wiley.com/doi/full/10.1002/2017WR022402

Session 3: Harnessing multiple sources of private finance

The session highlighted opportunities and challenges to mobilise different sources of finance in order to bridge the investment gap for achieving the objectives of the WFD. The session discussed examples and challenges related to the valuation of water and the generation of revenues streams. It then highlighted opportunities to tap into sustainable finance in relation to the new EU taxonomy. Lastly, it discussed the importance of an attractive risk-return profile to attract private investment.

Valuing water and generating revenue streams

Water related investments and particularly nature-based solutions (NbS) for water security deliver multiple benefits for a range of stakeholders. When monetised, these benefits can generate a revenue stream and mobilise additional private finance sources. Member States signalled high interest in these solutions.

The Nature Conservancy (TNC) supports analysis on how to monetise these benefits and sets up water funds to coordinate and pool the various stakeholders. Water funds can operate as coordination platforms and as collective investment mechanisms to mobilise upfront repayable finance as well as to generate continuous revenue streams to pay back investment in NbS for water security.

The Greater Cape Town Water Fund, for instance, financed the removal of invasive plant species, which lead to increased water supply that yielded in water savings two months worth of water. Other financing examples include the performance-based Environmental Impact Bond in Washington DC for storm water runoff, and the Netherland's Sovereign Green Bond for Natural Flood Management (see PowerPoint slides and resources further below). The Sustainable Water Impact Fund is another financing model that invests in rewetting measures in failing farms in Western United States, Australia and Chile, hence contributing to groundwater recharge. In California, recharging groundwater is valorised and financially remunerated, and thus provides a funding stream to repay the upfront investment cost. This example highlights the importance of a **conducive regulatory framework that supports the valorisation of accruing benefits,** which is the basis of effective financing. In this context, biodiversity credit markets were mentioned as another example of a regulatory setting that can help monetise benefits of NbS for water security.

TNC is currently preparing the first water fund in Europe in East Anglia, UK. First analyses on potential funding sources for the intervention found that more than 50 sources were assigned to NbS in a fragmented manner. **There is hence potential for better coordination of the funding sources into a single funding structure**. In the EU, for example, farmers need to apply for funding for environmental practices on an individual basis, whereas landscape level interventions (in coordination with other farmers) would be more effective. A more strategic coordination among actors and stakeholders to finance landscape-based interventions is hence vital.

Further, it was reported that stakeholders need reliable estimates on potential benefits before they commit to such a financing structure. **There is a need for methods and data to assess the benefits** relevant to a stakeholder, as well as performance records of successful examples.

While numerous successful examples exist, transaction costs of such platforms and financing models can be high. **Further efforts are needed to reduce transaction costs over time** and to establish mechanisms that do not only cover the initial investment but also serve as operational investment platform in the long run.

Attracting sustainable finance

Water-related investments have the potential to attract finance from private investors with an interest in sustainable investment opportunities. One example is the Austrian wastewater treatment plant upgrade, financed by EIB's Climate Awareness Bonds. The project proved compliance with climate objectives due to energy efficiency gains and renewable energy production, and was hence able to attract a dedicated EIB loan and commercial finance.

The EU taxonomy on sustainable finance is a framework that defines thresholds for projects and interventions to be considered sustainable. Water-related projects could gain visibility to new types of investors if they comply with the EU taxonomy's criteria. On the one hand, this could allow tapping into new sources of finance (e.g. climate finance), but on the other, might increase the administrative burden of reporting. While some participants were active in the consultation process of the taxonomy development, others were not familiar with the regulation and criteria related to water. **This highlights the need for better communication** of the taxonomy, better integration of all sectors in these endeavours as well as **capacity building for project developers and water managers to demonstrate compliance** with such criteria or contributions to other policy objectives (e.g. renewable energy production).

Improving the risk-return profile

The last topic discussed investment in water-related projects from an investor's view point. Private investors are primarily concerned with the risk-return profile of an investment and it is hence essential to 'build a narrative' for the investors – to prepare bankable projects with well-documented risks and returns. While finance is available for infrastructure, there might be limited investors' willingness to take on residual risk. In Romania, for example, private investors tend to not having an interest in investing in water-related projects. In order to attract private investors with varying risk appetites, **a combination of specific financing mechanisms, contractual arrangements and well-prepared projects is required**. Pooling mechanisms or de-risking arrangements can help improve the risk-return profile and render projects more attractive. Ring-fencing income flows can also provide investors security on predictable and stable revenues flows. Overall, there is a need for a better understanding and communication between the water and private investor community, and intermediaries can play a role in connecting these.

Resources shared by participants

Links on NbS for water security - The Nature Conservancy:

- Report: NbS for European Water Security; https://www.nature.org/en-us/what-we-do/our-insights/perspectives/nature-based-solutions-for-european-water-security/
- Biodiversity Net Gain in England, Developing Effective Market Mechanisms https://www.nature.org/content/dam/tnc/nature/en/documents/TNC_BiodiversityNetGain_England.pdf
- Report: Resilient European Cities: NbS for Clean Water: https://www.nature.org/en-us/what-we-do/our-insights/perspectives/resilient-european-cities-clean-water/
- UK Payments for Ecosystem Services: Best practice guide https://www.gov.uk/government/publications/payments-for-ecosystem-services-pes-best-practice-guide
- And Pilot projects

- https://www.gov.uk/government/publications/payments-for-ecosystem-services-review-of-pilot-projects-2011-to-2013
- Overview of UK Consultation on Biodiversity Net Gain Regulations and Implementations https://consult.defra.gov.uk/defra-net-gain-consultation-team/consultation-on-biodiversity-net-gain-regulations/
- Information on UK Environmental Bill including conservation covenants https://www.gov.uk/government/publications/environment-bill-2020/10-march-2020-nature-and-conservation-covenants-parts-6-and-7
- Policy Paper: Environmental land management schemes: payment principles (UK) https://www.gov.uk/government/publications/environmental-land-management-schemes-payment-principles
- And test and trials:
- https://www.gov.uk/government/publications/environmental-land-management-tests-and-trials
- Paper on Water Catchment management, abstraction and flooding: the case for a catchment system operator and coordinated competition (Professor Dieter Helm CBE)
- http://www.dieterhelm.co.uk/natural-capital/water/water-catchment/
- Vienna Wastewater Treatment upgrade: https://www.ebswien.at/klimaschutz/ *(available in German only)*
- Report 'The European environment – state and outlook 2020: knowledge for transition to a sustainable Europe' EEA https://www.eea.europa.eu/soer/2020
- Background information on EU Taxonomy: https://ec.europa.eu/info/business-economy-euro/banking-and-finance/sustainable-finance/eu-taxonomy-sustainable-activities_en

References

European Environment Agency (2022), *European Environment Agency, Indicators, Pesticides in rivers, lakes and groundwater*, https://www.eea.europa.eu/ims/pesticides-in-rivers-lakes-and (accessed on 2022). [2]

IEA (2022), *IEA*, https://www.iea.org/data-and-statistics/charts/share-of-russia-in-european-union-and-united-kingdom-gas-demand-2001-2021 (accessed on 2022). [3]

Nödler, K., T. Licha and D. Voutsa (2013), "Twenty years later – Atrazine concentrations in selected coastal waters of the Mediterranean and the Baltic Sea", *Marine Pollution Bulletin*, Vol. 70/1-2, pp. 112-118, https://doi.org/10.1016/j.marpolbul.2013.02.018. [1]

Notes

[1] Technical urgency is determined as the distance between the current probability of failure of the barrier and the standard applicable to that barrier.

[2] Transformation is required when exogenous conditions are changed to an extent where the system cannot maintain the same level of functions without a complete change of the system. Transformation can be achieved through additional connectivity to new supplies, restoring or resupply of water resources, changes in user consumptive behaviour, etc.

www.ingramcontent.com/pod-product-compliance
Lightning Source LLC
Chambersburg PA
CBHW061225240926
51846CB00006B/1359